Dead Birds Don't Sing But Witching Rods Talk

by Murray McGill

TEACH Services, Inc.
www.TEACHServices.com

Copyright © 2010 TEACH Services, Inc.
ISBN-13: 978-1-57258-628-4
Library of Congress Control Number: 2010930816

Cover artist - Gary Rolfe

The art depicts the circle of life, death, and immortality as represented
throughout history by sun and serpent - usually colored orange or gold.
The chickadee is perched on a twisted power stick or
Indian divining rod (see chapters 1 and 34).

Published by
TEACH Services, Inc.
www.TEACHServices.com

Dedication

This book is dedicated to six people:

1. To my wife, Linda, who still cries when she reads the third story.

2. To my son, Kevin, who kept telling me to write the book.

3. To Kevin's wife, Danelle, whose favorite story is "Man's Best Friend".

4. To my daughter, Lisa, who told me not to write the "Flatulence" story.

5. To Lisa's husband, Lee, who is no longer laughing about his cousin's Sasquatch encounter.

6. To Danny Shelton who kept asking on 3ABN television, "What do you have in your hand?" So I used what I had in *my* hand to write about the rod that Moses had in *his* hand.

Contents

Introduction

A few years ago I approached the newspaper in my town with an idea for a column that would consist of a wide-ranging mixture of stories, most of them local. The column would feature humorous and serious stories as well as wild and hard-to-believe stories but all of them—true stories.

The idea was accepted and this book is an extension of that idea. I have been told that one should not mix many different types of topics. But this book seeks to include a few stories for just about everybody. Some stories will evoke a chuckle; others will (hopefully) be thought provoking. A few stories may be disturbing and might challenge cherished ways of thinking.

This book draws on local and Native (Indian) stories that might have been passed over as legends from the past, when perhaps, there is more to the stories than meets the eye. The stories are not necessarily politically correct but I have attempted to tell them in a sensitive manner. If the reader does not like one story there will probably be another that he *will* appreciate.

Some of these stories will introduce topics from a new perspective and with a different twist. Some are Spiritual stories. There are philosophical and even religious concepts that can become exciting when absorbed through the medium of true and verifiable narrative.

A story which one reader might find almost unbelievable will bring relief to someone else. For example, I know that I will be hearing more Sasquatch stories after this book. Several of the stories that are recounted have never been told before or were told to very few people because they just seemed incredible beyond belief.

Dead birds don't sing and I know one little chickadee that never sang again after I put a bullet in its chest—the subject of the first story. *But witching rods talk* and that is one of the stories that might disturb and surprise, perhaps. The fact that witching rods can talk is something the Native people knew long before Europeans came on the scene. I leave you now to laugh a little, wonder a little, and think a lot.

1

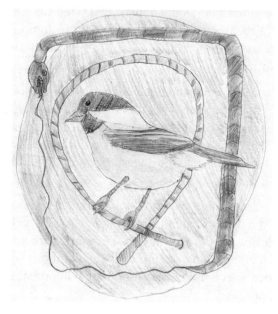

Chickadee on a Native "twisted power stick" against a backdrop
of a Sun disk and Ouroboros serpent - by Carlye Smedley

Chapter 1

Dead Birds Don't Sing

I believe most little boys are fascinated with guns and I was no exception. They are at once exciting, but also powerful and deadly. When in the fall the men slung rifles on their shoulders and trudged off in search of moose or bear, I and other little friends would gaze at the sleek weapons and wonder at their destructive power.

We often played "huntin" (as we called it) and killed many, many, ferocious grizzly bears. We also shot and ate many a moose, even though I was a vegetarian.

Some of the "big" boys got rifles of their very own—B.B. guns. How we little boys envied them! We begged to touch the guns and hold them.

I learned how to line the sights and squeeze the trigger at just the right moment. I promised myself that I would shoot only pop cans and bottles. None of them were safe; more "living" targets were only considered. I quickly became a very proficient marksman.

One day a little buddy came running and excitedly informed me that his dad had agreed to take us target shooting with a *big* gun—a .22 rifle. What excitement! And what an adrenalin rush as bottles and cans exploded off the fence posts.

We were out in rolling ranch country. Here and there were "gopher" or "ground squirrel" colonies. Need I say more? This was a *real* "huntin" expedition. I still remember the little squirrel standing so stiffly and erect beside his home in the ground. He was ready to sound a danger alarm but saw no need, as we were quite a distance from him.

My little friend, Jackie, could not conceal his pride for his dad as the gun was lifted and aimed. I, however, was suddenly seized with a mixture of fascination and horror as I realized that this splendid little creature was about to have its life snuffed out. I could hardly bear the suspense, and seconds seemed like hours. I wanted to scream "No!"

The shot rang out as the squirrel jerked in convulsive death. I was filled with instant remorse. And we just walked away and left the little creature lying there. It seemed so senseless. My mother had been right about guns.

Once should have been enough, but I went hunting one more time –*hunting* this time and not "huntin." That's because the boy who took me with his B.B. gun, was a *big* boy and he used the proper terminology. He was one of the older boys, very tough, and "with" it. To be invited to hunt with him was quite an honor.

We hadn't gone into the woods very far before we found our first living, moving targets. A flock of black-capped chickadees was flitting among some low bushes. My friend killed a little bird, and as it flopped lifeless to the ground, I was horrified. I couldn't stop myself from exclaiming, "You killed it!" He looked at me incredulously, and with some alarm, before handing me the gun. "Of course," he said, "we're hunting. Now it's your turn."

I'm sure he was afraid I was going to make trouble. The women frowned on the killing of defenseless little birds. And he was going to make certain that I stained my hands with blood. My lips would be

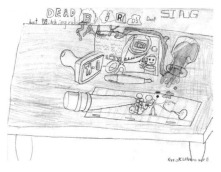

sealed if I shared in his guilt. He was correct in that, because I was too ashamed to tell anyone what happened next.

Against my better judgment, and while my friend looked on to make sure the grisly deed was accomplished, I took aim, and fired. I had considered "missing" on purpose but knew that the agony would only be prolonged.

There was a "puff" of downy feathers in the chest region of a chickadee, as my bullet found its mark. I felt like a murderer, and to add to my misery, the little bird did not die immediately, but fluttered helplessly and painfully about for a few moments.

I was sickened by what I had done. I gazed at the little feathered body with wings partially outstretched and head flopped awkwardly on the ground. I desired only to go home. Although I am a husband and father now, the horrible scene is still vivid in my memory, inscribed there through the eyes of a little 8-year-old boy.

I determined never to hunt for sport. Life was just too beautiful and precious. And I was convicted that God's creation was not to be mistreated or destroyed in this manner. It is sometimes necessary to kill, but I have never done so for fun. It is the "vibrancy" of life that brings me joy. And, "dead" birds don't sing.

Chapter 2

All in a Day's Fishing

A salmon seine net is about a quarter mile long and held up by floats, called corks. The web is sunk beneath the water by a lead line that stretches along the bottom of the net. The net is pulled into a circle and metal rings, attached to the lead line, are pulled up to the boat, thus trapping the fish.

One day the net was "pursed" and the rings, which were attached to the heavy lead line, were hanging on the hairpin. But the boat gave a heave, the rings fell into the water, and the hairpin shot backwards and up into the rigging.

I screamed a warning and dove for cover down by the drum. Jerry had been standing on the outside edge of the boat and the hairpin was about to make the return swing. He was confined by a scarcity of space. I kept yelling at him, so he took a flying leap out into the water. When we fished him out he said that I had been in his way and had taken the spot that he had wanted. I told him not to worry about the laughter from the crew; his life was much more important.

I went into the water once too. We often pushed our skiff off the back of the boat while someone snubbed the bowline and eased it off slowly. One day I was helping to push the skiff, thinking that my wife had the line snubbed. But she let it fly and the skiff went sailing full speed off the back of the boat and crashed into the water.

That would only have been mildly humiliating, as the skiff was partially submerged. Unfortunately, I was hanging onto the bow through the wild show and went sailing into the water with it. I was the skipper. The whole performance was staged in front of several other boats. My crew man, Lenny, laughed so hard and so long that it became irritating. But I got my revenge by way of a shark.

A salmon shark is the most active and voracious of our northern sharks; it looks like a great white shark. We caught a big one and we were gingerly trying to roll it off the stern, when it went berserk.

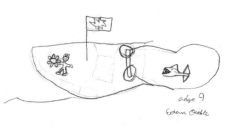

We all scattered as it thrashed and bit at anything within reach. Lenny became trapped and in his panic, he tried to climb the net that was rolled on the seine drum. But he could only get himself pulled up far enough to clear the deck and his butt was hanging down.

The shark's tail hit him repeatedly and Lenny couldn't see what was happening because his back was turned and he was desperately trying to keep his legs and body clear. All he could think of, as he was being thrashed, was that those wicked teeth were just about to sink into one of his cheeks. I gleefully told him later that the screaming was enough to make us think that his whole derriere had been torn off and swallowed.

Another of my crew, Gordie, told about his first day fishing herring. He went gillnetting with some rough and wild old-timers to the operation. Everything was pandemonium as the net was set out the first time. He was told to let the net slide through his spread legs, as sort of a guide, and then the anchor would be thrown out at the end.

He was a little guy and the big scotchman float at the end of the net got caught between his legs. He couldn't get free and the man running the boat just kept yelling at him to let it go. Amid all the noise and confusion, the lines stretched tight until he could hold on no longer.

Suddenly the net exploded up over the back of the boat and high into the air with him (in his bulky rain clothes) still sitting on the scotchman. What goes up must come down and although the water was bitterly cold, the damage to his ego was even worse.

Chapter 3

A Love Story

I was in love; I thought about her constantly and I must admit that I caught myself often dwelling on her considerable physical charms which first had caught my attention. And she could kiss rather passionately too. But there was more—I missed her, I was lonely and she was nearly one thousand miles removed.

I was working all summer in the woods to finance my next year of college. The wet days, which were often, were the most miserable. Consequently, my mind often tuned out and tuned "in" to much more pleasant things.

Etched in my memory is a certain day that found me walking in the rain and through very wet woods to the work site. We had about a half mile hike and although I was dressed in rain gear, I still got soaked even before reaching the logging area. I was grumpy and feeling sorry for myself.

I can clearly remember walking with my caulk boots across a log which spanned a rushing creek. On the other side the trail continued through some old-growth spruce trees. And then I became aware of the most beautiful and cheerful lilting melody filtering through the forest. The music slowly filled my being with wonder and awe; I had been so focused on the darkness and the rain that I had almost missed the magic of the moment.

How could any living creature possibly be happy, I wondered? But a little robin was. He was singing as if this day was the most glorious day of his life. And then I realized why - he was singing for his girlfriend—singing in the rain and his love for her lifted him above the dismal surroundings.

Many years before, William Wordsworth had written these words:

"I wandered lonely as a cloud
That floats on high oe'r vales and hills,
When all at once I saw a crowd,
A host, of golden daffodils;
Beside the lake, beneath the trees,
Fluttering and dancing in the breeze.

Continuous as the stars that shine
And twinkle on the Milky Way,
They stretched in never-ending line
Along the margin of a bay:
Ten thousand saw I at a glance,
Tossing their heads in sprightly dance.

The waves beside them danced; but they
Outdid the sparkling waves in glee:
A poet could not but be gay,
In such jocund company:
I gazed - and gazed—but little thought
What wealth the show to me had brought:

For oft, when on my couch I lie
In vacant or in pensive mood,
They flash upon that inward eye
Which is the bliss of solitude;
And then my heart with pleasure fills,
And dances with the daffodils."

That little robin caused my heart also, to dance. Suddenly the grey day was eclipsed by a brightness that flooded my inner being. My girl may have been a thousand miles away but I could sing for her too. I composed a poem in my mind and wrote it out later. I wondered if I would ever have the opportunity or the nerve to recite it to the one I loved. I even came up with a tune that matched somewhat the actual melody that the robin had been singing. Eventually, the sun burst forth in all its glory but it really didn't matter anymore.

Some weeks later, my girl drove 700 miles and flew another 300 just to see me. I was excited but also a little nervous. She put me at ease with her kisses which were every bit as good as I had remembered. Somewhere along the way I took her for a romantic boat ride that she still talks about. We found a remote beach and explored it together, hand-in-hand. It was a brilliant, gorgeous day and that evening a full moon rose after the sun had disappeared beneath the watery horizon.

As the outboard hummed and we shared our thoughts, I mentioned that I had written a poem. She wanted to hear it but I wasn't so sure. She coaxed and finally I overcame my inhibitions and recited these words into her ear:

Robin Redbreast sings
And my, oh how this valley rings!
With his song of love
Bursting from that branch above.

Sing on my little friend
And lift your head up high
Oh let the whole world know…
I feel the same way too.

9

Someone sitting near
She loves to hear you loud and clear
So let your feelings out,
You've something to be proud about.

Sing on my little friend
And lift your head up high,
Oh let the whole world know...
I feel the same way too.

Yes, let the whole world know...
I feel the same way too.

I can hardly believe that I also sang the "Robin Redbreast" poem to her. The outboard continued humming, the waves splashed against the boat and the moon seemed to shine more brightly then ever before. I stole a timid glance to my side and noted tears streaming down the face of that beautiful young woman. As she snuggled closer I knew that I had made the right decision.

She threw her arms around me and kissed me. Oh how I like to be smothered with her sweet and tender, feminine love. Thank God for forests with robins!

Do you remember watching from a distance
And wishing you could feast your eyes more closely?
Do you remember the graceful figure that so attracted you
back then?
And when you passed her and then looked back,
Do you remember how she was just as pretty from behind?
Her movements, her smile, and her laugh –
Do you remember watching?

Do you remember waiting to meet with her,
How you wanted to appear so casual
As you planned and calculated every move?
Do you remember the joy of simple talking
And how the hours sped swiftly by?

Do you remember waiting for the opportunity
To ask her for the first official date?
Do you remember waiting?

Do you remember touching her with your eyes
And later with your lips?
Do you remember how eagerly she responded?
Do you remember the touching of two minds
And the sharing of new thoughts and feelings?
Could you ever forget the touching?

Do you remember the many firsts?
Can you still remember
The first time you laid eyes on her?
Do you remember the first full night together?
Do you relive your honeymoon from time to time?
Do you remember how both of you
Thought your joy would never end?
Do you? Do you remember?

Chapter 4

Abducted

When I was about 11 years old, my grandfather lived in White
Rock, B.C. overlooking Semiahmoo Park, near the Pacific Ocean.
Some other relatives lived several miles away, on Zero Avenue, which
ran along the border between the United States and Canada.

My brother and I sometimes walked from the park, along the
beach to the Peace Arch (marking the boundary between Canada and
the U.S.) and then up to Zero Avenue. In the winter and spring the
beach was deserted and very few people lived along that stretch.

One Sunday afternoon I walked the beach by myself, which wasn't
unusual, as I liked to bird-watch and look for crabs etc. Somewhere

along the way I saw a distant figure and our paths eventually crossed. As I think back, this man very cleverly made it appear that we just *happened* to bump into each other. He seemed to be looking for crabs and did not noticeably look my way until we met.

He was very cordial, casual and disarming. He showed me how to safely pick up large crabs and talked about a variety of subjects, including religion. He told me which denomination he belonged to and in the process he learned a lot about me. Then he told me about a deserted cabin nearby that had old coins strewn about. We went to his car so that he could get his boots. He acted like he had all the time in the world.

We had just entered the trees, when he reached over and very firmly grasped my wrist; and I knew that I was in big trouble. As he forced me along he asked if I knew what a homosexual was. I didn't.

He said a homosexual was someone who liked boys. That didn't help. The many definitions regarding gay, homo, soft porn, hard porn, child porn, X, XXX, uni, bi, tri, or whatever else there might be had not yet been invented.

He firmly told me to unbuckle my belt. I refused. His attitude quickly changed and became frightening. He attempted to force my compliance but I resisted, so he then threatened to cut me up. And he said he was going to put the "sleeper" hold on me until I passed out and then he would follow through with his threats.

I appealed to his sense of religion and justice. I appealed to his sense of mercy. Nothing worked and in spite of my best efforts to avoid it, I began to cry. In my mind I pleaded for divine help. I made foolish promises to God about how I was going to change my life and study my Bible etc. (I've since learned that what God really wants is just our day-to-day honest loyalty and friendship; the rest falls into place)

My captor put a double arm-lock around my throat and began to choke me. I got light headed but I could still breathe. Up until that time I had not resisted with my full strength for fear of what might happen if I was unsuccessful. But I decided that if I should feel myself starting

12

to pass out or if this man should stab or hurt me, I would attack him with everything I had.

Through the trees, I remember seeing two girls pushing their bikes along a trail but I couldn't speak. The man had one hand roughly clamped over my mouth. I also remember being held, briefly, in a way that no man should ever dare to do.

The molester suddenly fled through the trees, wildly looking one way and then the other. It was strange, because up until that moment, he had been so calm and in control. I was molested but I was not raped. I may have been an ill-informed kid with no inkling as to what that man's intentions were, but even then, I was impressed with the feeling that he fled before finishing whatever it was he had in mind for me.

I dove into the bushes and ran through the trees. I made my way to the Peace Arch, all the while checking to make sure that I wasn't being followed or ambushed. I briefly considered stopping at the Canadian Customs to tell an officer about what had happened but discarded that idea. I think I was too embarrassed.

I ate the evening meal with my family and relatives, watched television, and made a special effort to appear normal and relaxed. I said nothing until I was ready to go to bed. Then I asked my mother what a homosexual was. She asked, "Why?" and I haltingly told her the basic details of my experience.

Her reaction was the worst part of the whole ordeal. She burst into tears, began to tremble and shake, and sort of collapsed into an armchair. And I wished that I had kept my big mouth shut. I was glad that my dad was away at a logging camp because I think that his anger and unceasing questions and instructions would have made things worse.

Later, a detective came to question me. I told him that the man's clothing was just normal, no particular color that I could remember. His shoes were black, or maybe brown. I didn't know what kind of car he drove even though I had leaned against it while he changed his footwear. And I couldn't recall the color. I did believe the man to be about thirty years of age, with a narrow face, and noticeable pimples or zits. That was it. I did not hear if he was ever picked up.

From that day, things changed for me. I became more observant and less trusting. I tried to always be aware of what was happening around me. If I was the least bit suspicious I noted things like clothing, color, mannerisms, and license plates. I now realized that the nicest people just might be the most dangerous killers or molesters, in disguise. And religion, I noted, could be the perfect cover.

Unfortunately, we live in a world where children have to be taught about the danger that can come from an increasingly younger and younger age group. I've used this story to educate my own kids, as I tried to warn them without causing undo anxiety or worry. I have also tried to learn from my experience in other ways.

Parents cannot assume that nothing like my experience has happened, or will happen, to their children. Open communication must be encouraged and parents should be careful not to over react if something ugly does take place. Be careful about being too graphic when describing potential dangers but at the same time, it doesn't hurt to point out the kinds of situations that might need to be discussed, should they ever occur.

In my case, it was a couple of weeks later that we visited my grandpa again. And I told my mother that I was walking that same beach and would meet everybody later. She gave me a quizzical look and asked, "Are you sure?" And then, after a pause and with a certain tonal reluctance, she said, "Okay." And I have always been thankful that she gave me the opportunity to deal with my anger at my previous naiveté.

Chapter 5

Flatulence

I would not say that the North Island has more flatulence than the larger cities to the south of us. In fact, I think that our good local politicians and mayors would agree that when it comes to important issues such as environment, land use, logging, commercial fishing, and maybe even some aboriginal issues, the city dwellers seem all too often to be filled almost to overflowing with the stuff.

What is flatulence? My father (now deceased) simply and flatly, point-blank, called it gas. And he should have known, because all too often he suffered with the condition. But I think my mother would have said that he did not always suffer quietly. And at times, he would chuckle, much to my mother's disgust, so to say that he suffered, would perhaps be missing the mark.

I think my father can take the credit for my sister's laying down the law to her new husband before any symptoms even developed. My wife remembers *her* dad (also a logger like my father) somewhat similarly. When conditions warranted it, her mother would put on her stern face and icily tell the kids, "Don't laugh."

The difference between rural people and city dwellers, is, that city folk tend to keep it all inside. Country folk, like North Islanders, you know—(Fi-Lo-Mi)* types, tend to harmlessly release measured amounts of flatulence into the atmosphere. Maybe it has to do with the abundance of fresh air and wide-open spaces.

I should however, point out, that for some unknown reason, females almost never experience this problem. But my dad said that when he was young, he had a friend named Pappy Switzer (I think).

Switzer reported that once he had been on a date with a pretty girl, and as the evening shadows fell, a thunderstorm developed. It was quite romantic really, and the girl held Switzer close, as the lightning flashed and the thunder roared. Unbeknownst to Switzer, this gal had one of those very rare conditions.

It was very fortunate that the wild elements of the evening conveniently masked the problem. According to my dad, who simply repeated what Switzer had reported, this girl became careless.

After one particularly loud clap of thunder, she said, "My, that was a big one!" And Switzer immediately replied, "Yes, and it smells like it hit an outhouse." That's according to my dad, according to Switzer.

Flatulence can sometimes backfire as a certain fisherman found out. Gary and one of his deckhands had just tied the boat up one evening, and after cleaning up, they were proceeding up the ramp to their vehicles. Gary stopped momentarily and his friend, thinking he was right behind him, and in fact, hearing footsteps, let loose with one of his most tuneful pieces of flatulent melody.

He then stopped, doubled up with laughter, and without looking back, yelled, "How did you like that one, eh?" But his smile froze when an unknown, and very irritated, feminine voice replied, "Thank you very much!" He was still apologizing and wishing to die, when Gary caught up with him.

Hopefully it was more bearable, when after some heavy arm-twisting, Gary told the story one more time, at his friend's wedding.

*Fi-Lo-Mi, in Port Hardy-eze is short for fishing, logging, mining.

Chapter 6

Rip It Up

I generally send the editor four to six articles ahead and then review them from time to time and change or adapt as conditions warrant. I was somewhat hesitant about the "Flatulence" and "Dam Beavers" stories.

My daughter, who is away at college studying Organic chemistry and other exciting subjects, reinforced that hesitance. When she heard about my proposal, she told my wife, "Mom, do not, I repeat, do not, let Dad print that flatulence article in the paper!" But she also said that her class had had a humorous, *scientific* article on the causes of flatulence.

From time to time I intend to write some very different, and hopefully, thought-provoking articles. And some of them, at least from my point of view, will be deadly serious. But a column called "True Tales" leaves a wide variety of options available.

My daughter found her scientific article to be hilarious, but apparently my humble story was not. At any rate, I decided several weeks ago, that I would not mix my sick humor with serious subjects. And I reassured my daughter that the two stories would not be published.

I sent some replacement stories to the editor and went on a holiday with my wife. So I was surprised, upon my return, to see that the story I thought ripped up, had come back to haunt me, under the title, "Letting One Rip…"

I need to let my dear readers know (any of you who might actually read my column) that I do not choose the titles. The editor picks something that suits his fancy and sounds like a newspaper.

I would never have chosen the title, "Letting One Rip." I had a much more cultured and refined title. My story was simply and benignly entitled, "Flatulence." And since the story ended with an introduction to the other story I had decided against, (Dam Beavers) I guess we will have to go with that one too.

I checked the "sent items" on my computer screen, and saw that I had indeed sent two messages to the editor telling him to clear his computer and go with the new stories. And we had also talked by telephone, but Mark somehow neglected to clear his screen of the old e-mail information.

My daughter called last night and I was unable to break the news to her. I am asking any of you who might know her, to please let the flatulence story float off into the atmosphere, out of sight and out of mind.

Next week's article is actually a letter, apparently written by a man to Michigan's Department of Environment Quality. He was accused of constructing a poorly built wood-debris dam without authorization. He pointed out, that not only did they send the registered letter to the wrong landowner, but they also had the wrong contractors; it was the beavers that were responsible. This is why a letter was sent to the dam department.

If you wish to read the humorous true story, go to an internet search engine and punch in the words "Dam Beavers" or "Steve Tvedten"

Chapter 7

Fishing Tales

In 25 years, I have never caught a cormorant. They are wary and cautious and observant. But the murres and auklets (ocean birds) often try to *dive* out of the net, rather than *fly* out. We try to avoid them, but if any do become tangled in the web, we pick them out and throw them into the air.

The murres almost always scramble over the corks at the last minute, but the (catch this) rhinoceros auklets, can be really exasperating. They have a little horn on their bill (hence, the name) and they use their short wings to fly under the water. They are very tough, and have on occasion, been wrapped on the drum, only to come to life like angry little hornets when the net is set again.

Alvin worked for my brother Gary, on the boat, "Oceanaire." One day he sort of became a "rhinoceros auklet." The Oceanaire was pulling a massive set of sockeye salmon aboard. The hydraulics, drum, and boom, strained as thousands of fish slowly rolled over the stern. With a whoosh, that all fishermen will understand, the fish filled the stern area to overflowing and slid under the drum.

In the excitement no one noticed that Alvin was missing. But then they heard a squeak from somewhere under the fish. Alvin had been caught in the "whoosh" and was stuck under all the slime and scales. He couldn't move and could hardly talk.

Poor Alvin sounded like a rhinoceros auklet, and when he was finally dug out, he looked like one too. And although he was every bit as angry as a rhinoceros auklet, he was actually a very bruised, wet, and slimy human being.

Alvin's brother, Lenny, worked for me. He operated the deck controls, winches, and running line. He backed the "running line" off and opened the hatches for the fish to slide into the chilled water. A portion of his job was done while the rest of the crew dumped the fish from the net and prepared it for another set.

One day, we too, had a big set. After helping the crew get things ready on the back deck, and with fish flipping all over the boat, I was rushing forward to the wheelhouse. But I heard a faint, little voice yelling, "Help, help!"

The heavy hatch covers were all in place. There was no way that anyone could have fallen into the holding area under the deck, but the voice sounded as if it was coming from beneath the boat.

I looked all over, and although I knew it made no sense whatsoever, I even looked under a piece of equipment known as the deck winch. Then I yelled, "Where are you?" And Lenny's voice replied, "Down in the hatch!"

I strained to lift the heavy lid, and there he was, hanging by his arms, and suspended in ice water up to his chest. It seems that he had stepped on one of the covers that was not completely closed, and it had flipped him down below and then slid back into place, leaving him in utter darkness and freezing cold.

But the worst was yet to come. Apparently, when I grabbed hold of the top of his rain pants and with a surge of energy, yanked him to freedom, I did great damage to the lower parts of his anatomy.

Those parts that made him decidedly male had already been frozen, and then I crushed them. He does, however, have two children now, so thankfully, the damage was not permanent.

Chapter 8

They Cry

Pacific white-sided dolphins are playful, intelligent, and acrobatic, but they are not so smart when it comes to nets. The dall's porpoises, on the other hand, can fish right alongside us and almost never get caught. They are the little black-and-whites that look like miniature orcas.

It is astounding to see the orcas (killer whales) swim into nets, around nets and under them, with no concern whatsoever. The tourists might worry, but the orcas know exactly what they're doing. And the smaller porpoises have adapted well too.

On several occasions though, I've caught the pacific white-sided dolphins even when I opened the seine net to let them out. I was fishing after dark one time and thought I saw some quick splashes that could have been rocks. The chart showed nothing unusual but I closed up anyway.

We were drumming the net aboard when several dolphins streaked across the surface and hit the web. There was nothing we could do except carefully bring them aboard and untangle and roll them out. I will never forget the way they loudly cried in distress and confusion. There was no mistaking it. They did not fight or make it difficult for us at all. They simply cried and cried as if they thought it was all over for them.

Each dolphin was carried to the edge of the boat and carefully slipped back into the ocean. Finally, all of the heart-rending pleas for mercy were silenced as they swam away.

They Cry

The harbor porpoises behave differently, again. A few years ago there was one that could be seen day after day in Port Hardy's inner harbor. But these porpoises are quiet and travel singly or in small loose groups. They surface quickly and quietly without any splashing, and because they are dark in color, can be easily missed even though they might be right under one's nose.

If you watch closely, on a calm day, you can sometimes see them at Storie's beach. You stand a better chance if you walk along the water's edge at a low tide and look out to sea. Often, if you *think* you might have seen a dark back roll on the surface, just keep watching, and you might see it again.

We caught one once and we didn't know it was in the net until it came aboard. It did not cry at all, but it went absolutely berserk. It thrashed and beat frantically with such powerful blasts, that we could not get close. It tore a tiny wound in its dorsal fin and that was its undoing. There was blood everywhere. When we finally got it back in the water, I could see bursts of blood with each heartbeat, as it swam away.

My dad once wounded a deer with a shotgun. He said that not only did it cry heart-rending sobs, but also tears actually rolled out of its big brown eyes as it watched him helplessly. It was his first and last hunting experience.

One other time he saw something similar with rats, of all creatures! They had become trapped in a grain barrel and were jumping frantically against the sides, but stopped when he peered in. They quietly stared back at him as he and they analyzed the situation.

He went to get the dog and he said you never heard such wailing and screeching the moment he left. Although they had been quietly leaping before, they now knew that their plight was known, and they sensed correctly, that their lives were about to end in violent death.

Chapter 9

Crying With The Porpoises

I have somewhat to say about the editor's choice of a title for my last week's column—"Fishing nets take toll on marine mammals." Jumpin Rhinoceros Auklet!! Have mercy. I'm still a sometimes-commercial fisherman and have friends in the industry.

The story was about grief and emotion in animals and included examples in sea creatures, a deer, and even some rats. I would have preferred something like "Shotgun blast causes deer to weep" or even "Psychic rats wail and screech as they foresee death." As a fisherman, and not an editor, I might have chosen something like "Orcas and porpoises adapt well to fishing nets."

But as I reviewed my story, I decided that parts of it were poorly written. Some things are learned in school, and some things are learned in the school of hard knocks. I was too frightened to take speech class, did not like English, and practiced only the basic writing that went with it. Does that help?

For clarification, let me explain that when I wrote about some dolphins that "cried and cried as if they knew it was all over for them," in actuality, they swam away alive and well when "all of the crew helped to carry each one to the side and slip it back into the ocean."

In twenty-five years of fishing I have caught several dolphins on only three occasions. And I expect that many, if not most, of my fellow fishermen friends have a better track record than mine. Although I wrote about a harbor porpoise that probably died, I do not know that for sure. One possible casualty—that's my story, and I'm sticking to it.

My type of fishing is called seining. The net is sometimes referred to as a "purse seine" because the net is pulled into a circle and then the bottom is closed or "pursed" shut and pulled alongside the boat. As one end of the net is drummed aboard, the circle gets smaller and smaller until the fish are trapped in the bunt end. With salmon, we used to pull the fish aboard, but now all seine boats brail them out with a big dip net and quickly sort the weaker species so that they can be returned, alive, to the water.

The net is made of heavy web that can be seen by fish and mammals. The idea is to trap the fish before they back out or swim around the ends. Porpoises gather information about the nets by echolocation. They have a sonar system that bounces sound waves through the water.

The orcas and porpoises maneuver among the nets with ease but the sports fisher people often drive their boats into the surface lines. And sometimes they get their propellers caught in the web. I expect that some of these fisher folk, in their concern for the whales, neglect to practice their own due care and diligence.

Some mammals enter the nets on purpose. I once hit a sea lion over the head a few times after it followed me around and even jumped over the corks, in order to help himself to the fish that were within the net. I explained to my little boy that the lion was getting a spanking. He understood, in theory at least, what that was all about.

On another note, some readers might remember the ill-fated "flatulence" story. My good friend, Ron Johnston, spilled the beans. He subtly hinted to my daughter, on her first morning home, that she might enjoy her dad's last few articles. Life can be hard, very, very hard.

Chapter 10

Have Faith My Dear

I am a commercial fisherman and the skipper of a seine vessel. My wife fishes with me, but in moments of weakness, she tells me that she wishes she had married a farmer. (Farmers tend to keep their feet on solid ground.)

Recently, she came up to the wheelhouse to tell me how much she *hated* fishing. I could hear some pots and pans clashing together on the galley floor and she had good reason to complain. Before she could get on the "farmer thing", I said to her with mock intensity, "Linda, where is your faith?"

She knew I was referring to a Bible story where Jesus says words like that to some fishermen who were caught with him in a violent storm. In the story, he calls out to the storm to be quiet and there is instant calm. In fact, the story seems to suggest that these men were as fearful of the unusual quiet as they had been of the raging squall. They talk among themselves in fear and amazement saying, "Who is this man that even the wind and the waves obey his voice?"

I remember another time when my wife was trying to reassure her parents who were with us on the boat. She had just finished telling them not to worry and that the storm outside was *nothing* when we dropped into a trough with a crash! As the unfriendly sea obliterated our view of anything familiar, she screamed at me to slow down, thus betraying her *true* feelings. In the chaos that followed, one parent stumbled to a bunk and the other became violently ill. My wife's little nephew loudly reported every time "Grandpa throwed up."

There is a book titled *Dangerous Waters* by Keith Keller, which tells of wrecks and rescues off the B.C. coast. I am in the first story and it brings back memories of a time when *I* was very frightened. I remember trying to keep the tremor out of my voice as I gave the particulars of another boat's capsize to the Canadian Coast Guard.

As the skipper on the 58-foot seine boat "Western Hunter", I was traveling up the west coast of Vancouver Island with another seine boat "Miss Joye" operated by Bruce Rafuse. The date was October 11, 1984 and on this night seven vessels capsized and five lives were lost when a storm struck earlier and with more violence than was expected.

I remember feeling envious of two boats that were jogging behind Brooks Peninsula, but the four people on these boats lost their lives when their vessels literally blew over. Apparently, this is an area where the "lee" isn't always safe, as violent wind seems to increase speed off the mountain.

Ken Datwiler on the "Lady Val II" was unable to beat his way in behind Brooks Peninsula to join his friends. He was in big trouble, proceeding towards Winter Harbor very slowly with Bruce following closely. Ken had a survival suit on, but not zipped up and was waiting for the inevitable. He actually told Bruce to carry on and save himself.

I was in trouble too. Earlier in the day, a large seine boat, the "Ocean Invader," had passed me, heading in the opposite direction. Hours later, I heard that this boat was heading for shelter with huge seas breaking over the cabin. I was passing Cape Cook and realized that the Ocean Invader's problems would soon be mine, as the storm approached my stern

I had two tanks ballasted with seawater and all my gear was tied down securely. The boom was lowered and tightened over the net and skiff. I flicked the dial on my V.H.F. radio to the weather channel, and did not like the upgraded "Storm Warning." And when I went out on deck, I was alarmed at the new intensity of the wind.

Soon my fears were confirmed. A violent wave washed over the boat and shifted the net to one side. The water in the ballast tank lifted the heavy metal lid and the wind caught the edge and flipped it across the deck. I foolishly ran out to tie a rope on this hatch cover, when another wave washed over the boat and nearly took me with it! I tied a safety line on myself and saved the cover. Water slopped out of the open hatch making our list worse. One side of the boat was buried under water. (Because the hatches could be completely flooded, I had not been concerned with bolting them down). I thought the danger would be from water coming in, not water sloshing out.

Our rolling caused bilge alarms to scream, jarring my nerves further. We weren't sinking, but rather, the violent action simply caused the safety floats to flip, thus triggering the alarm switches. I went below to check and got sick from diesel fumes (my crew was already sick and barely coping).

One of my deckhands, who was out with us for the first time, asked a question that we still chuckle about. He did not want to appear too concerned so he asked if he should be frightened yet. Before I could answer, another crewman asked if he should get the survival suits and I said "Yes."

My radar quit me for the first time ever, and the compass swung wildly as we were tossed and flipped every which way. So I thought

I would watch the wave direction (the wind was from the southeast). But the sea was so violent, everything looked the same and I found myself going in opposite directions and around in circles and all this happened at the same time.

I remember receiving a phone call from Ken Knopp who skippered a boat called the "Cap Rouge." I told him it was very nasty; not nice at all. I should have said, "One boat struggling to stay afloat, not sure about ourselves, getting worse."

At one point, my mouth became so dry that I left the wheel temporarily to get a drink. When I told Bruce later, he laughed and said his mouth had been so dry he could hardly swallow.

When the "Lady Val II" went over, my heart sank. I knew there was no chance of finding Ken Datwiler in such horrific seas and poor visibility, but I also knew we couldn't leave him. I prayed. Bruce says he told the Lord that for all our sakes we needed help desperately. One of my crew verbalized for all of us, "That guys a goner; we need to be thinking about ourselves."

I remember climbing to the bridge and hanging on desperately while scanning with the searchlight. The howling of the wind in the rigging prevented me from hearing the engine. Bruce had mentioned that Datwiler might have let his net go and I saw phantom nets and ropes everywhere. To make sure that the propeller hadn't stalled in a tangle, I would hit the throttle and watch for black exhaust smoke. When the wind was blasting our side, it took about half throttle just to change heading, and the extra lean was unnerving.

One image that burned itself in my mind was of a massive rolling wave much higher than the boat. In the darkness, I could see the white crest coming like a moving mountain. My heart nearly stopped, but somehow the boat rose up like a cork, to the top of the roller, before plunging down the other side.

The story of how Bruce and his deckhand rescued Datwiler is astounding (get the book *Dangerous Waters*) Datwiler was pretty well *finished* after twenty minutes, but upon rescue needed a smoke. Bruce was amazed that Datwiler had grabbed a new pack of cigarettes when fleeing his boat, and told him, "Now, that's a true smoker!"

26

Bruce had radar but no chart for Winter Harbor. I had a chart but no radar, so we helped each other limp into port. The crashing waves caused us to imagine rocks everywhere. Daylight was breaking when we reached harbor and sheets of water were blowing across the bay.

Datwiler later went to the pub in Port Hardy to celebrate "life." Bruce wasn't there but Bob Charlie phoned with the news that he was the most popular guy in the pub—the title of Keith Keller's story in "Dangerous Waters."

Bruce and I have often reviewed our experience together. We wonder what became of Ken Datwiler. And we wonder if Ken feels as strongly as we do, that our appointment with death was delayed through divine intervention. Life is precious, and time; especially *extra* time is a most valuable commodity.

Chapter 11

Danger at Sea

I previously related how my boat was able to play a part in the rescue of a man in the terrible fall storm of 1984. On that scary night I had a new man on board and he was nervously watching us for signs of panic. At one point, because he did not know what the norm was, he asked, "Should I be frightened?" About the same time, a seasoned crewman asked if he should get the survival suits and I replied with a simple, "Yes." The new man had very little to say the rest of the night but now, many years later, he reminds me of this experience every time I see him.

Another time we were fishing closer to home and had some visitors aboard. When we towed the two ends of the net together, the boat would lean. I could see the visitors watching us closely for any signs of alarm, so I ran to the far side of the top deck and stretched my body way out over the opposite side as I had seen sail boaters do. I tried to look panic stricken.

Our guests quickly joined me to prevent the boat from capsizing. But soon they noticed that the rest of the crew were doing nothing to help and that they were in fact, laughing. So they took a closer look at my expression and decided that it was insincere, whereupon they sat down and shook their heads in disgust, as they plotted revenge.

Commercial fishing is a dangerous occupation and I often remind the crew of pressure points and hazardous areas on the boat. But it is easy to become complacent and forgetful. I was looking back one day, while towing on the net, and thinking that my wife was not sitting in a safe area. Suddenly, there was a loud bang and at the same instant; she dropped over the edge of the boat.

Even though it was too quick for the eye to see, I knew instantly that the end of the net had ripped out and that the nylon tow line, with its steel shackle and hook, had recoiled and hit her in the head. She would have fallen into the water except that her feet became tangled in some hydraulic hoses.

I know now how it feels to see someone you love killed in front of your very eyes. I still remember the awful hollow weight in my chest as I made my way down, to what I thought, was her lifeless body.

And I also will never forget the flicker of hope when I found that she was still breathing. On closer examination, I realized that the spliced eye of the towline had let loose and the actual tow hook was still hanging in the end of the net. She had been struck a glancing blow just above her ear.

Linda regained consciousness and spent the night in the hospital because her speech and thinking was confused. She has suffered headaches periodically, but is once again, very feisty and alive. And I am so thankful to have someone to fight with.

Chapter 12

Dog People

I used to chuckle at those people who took their dogs with them in the car or boat. I told my family that cars, boats, and houses were definitely off limits to any dog that we should ever hypothetically acquire if we should possibly move to a farm or country setting. I thought I spoke firmly.

But my wife had a master plan that I knew nothing about. First she used the diplomatic approach. "Ask your father," she said to my son. (She had already smuggled a kitten into the house)

When I remained firm, she took the kids for a trip to see grandpa. Then she had him tell me that a little puppy had turned up. It and the boy had bonded, he said, and it would be awful to break them apart. He didn't have to tell me who would be the bad guy if I still said no.

Grandpa was quite proud of himself for finding such a wonderful free dog until he talked to the veterinarian. The vet said that he hoped no money had been spent on the supposedly part Australian sheep dog.

Grandpa helped the dog get into the house too, although he had never allowed animals in his own home and had gone on and on about it. I really had to grit my teeth when "Sport" began taking car and boat trips with us.

One day the dog became deathly ill. Not only had he chased the rocks that my boy had thrown, but he had swallowed them too. The operation cost $800 but no cost was too great for a boy's dog, my wife and her father said.

When the same thing happened again, I said that was it. Grandpa said to try castor oil. We forced lots of the stuff down the little dog's throat and amazingly, everything slipped free.

Our next door neighbors, the Downeys, owned Buster, a big golden retriever. Both dogs liked to play tug-o-war but Sport got very jealous if the other dog got too much attention. One day I had both of them tugging on a rag and I was egging them on.

Sport couldn't stand it and attacked his friend, grabbing him by some loose hanging fur. Buster saw red and ferociously tried to get revenge on the smaller dog. But he couldn't get hold of Sport who was hanging on for dear life as he was tossed around in a circle. They both acted sheepish when I hollered, "Hey, it's just a game; calm down now, you two."

Sport appeared to be the picture of obedience until one day as we were driving away, I glanced in the rear view mirror and there he was high-tailing it across to the Thornburns on the other side of the street. When we returned, I checked the mirror again and this time he was streaking back home and around the opposite side of the house in order to greet us as we drove into the garage. That way it looked as if he had been home the whole time.

I teased him and he teased the cat. It became impossible to open the treat door without him knowing. Even when sleeping, one ear was cocked for treats or tricks.

He seemed like a wimp, so I donned a Halloween mask, one day, and pretended to attack his little master. He came after me but seemed thoroughly embarrassed when I removed the disguise.

He died like a tough and loving little trooper when he became sick with some kind of poisoning. And then I actually shed a tear for the useless little rascal.

Chapter 13

At the Zoo

I've heard it said that a good way to get everyone's attention is to tell a narrative or explain a prin ciple on a child's level. Perhaps that is why "the children's corner" is such a popular weekly segment at my church. And maybe that is why I remember these animal stories—beginning with the story of Susie's encounter with the lions.

Her mother gave careful instructions about staying together and obeying the signs. As they viewed the lions, she pointed to the instructions that said to stay behind the zoo's fenced area and not to feed the animals.

The lions were lazily lying in the sun and didn't appear to be interested in the people and they certainly did not look very dangerous. The family moved on to the reptile building; Susie's mother became absorbed with reading the information about some of the creatures and the children became bored.

The girl and some friends returned to the lion cage for one more look. Unfortunately, she forgot her mother's instructions and climbed over the little fence and crossed a shallow moat to approach the cage area. A lion walked over and suddenly reached through the bars, clamping Susie tightly against the cage. It hurt, and she screamed, as other people watched helplessly.

Her mother came running, jumped the fence, and tried to make the lion release its grip on her daughter, but it was too powerful. So in desperation, she removed her high-heeled shoe and hit the lion's paw as hard as she could. The lion was startled and released its grip just long enough for the girl to collapse into her mother's arms.

The moral and lesson centered on obedience to parents who usually know best just as our heavenly Father also knows what's best for us.

Another story involved a monkey who liked to tease a certain lazy crocodile. The croc didn't seem to notice and appeared to be sleeping with its mouth open. The monkey teased and taunted and threw items from a tree - it looked so funny. When there was no response, the monkey gingerly moved out on a low, overhanging branch. What was the matter with that stupid crocodile? Was it really sleeping?

What happened next was a horrific surprise. The monkey made just one little, tiny slip but the crocodile instantly exploded forward and snapped those big jaws shut—end of that sad tale, except for the moral—don't play with sin; Satan is very patient.

Then there was the elephant that sprayed mud all over the people to show his unhappiness at being separated from an elephant friend. And another story explained how llamas could disgorge their stomach contents and spit the whole mess with great force and accuracy.

The woman who told that particular story talked from experience. Some people before her had upset a llama and she did not know that it was very angry. She also did not know about its unique ability to get even. Her outing at the zoo turned sour when a full stomach load hit her in the head and dripped all the way down to her shoes.

Because I had heard the children's story, I started to smile when "America's Funniest Home Videos" showed a little girl slapping a llama's nose. The scene showed the mother reprimanding the child before they approached the llama again. Then the camera jerked and went blank to the sound of screaming as the final shot showed a big, ugly, stomach barf - right in the face of the little gal. I leave you to figure out the moral to the story.

Chapter 14

Bears

On Vancouver Island there are lots of bears but recently I saw a large, brown bear and decided it must be a cinnamon "black." Now, with the news that a grizzly was shot in our area, I wonder.

Many years ago some of us went speeding (with a boat) up to a mother grizzly and her cubs. They ran into the trees but in a few moments the mother returned and charged down to the beach. Had we not been in the boat, there probably would have been quite a "scene."

Khutz Inlet is a beautiful wild place up the coast and across from the old Butedale cannery. A large glacier river empties into the head of the inlet where there are acres of tidal grass flats. Wolves, grizzlies and mountain goats inhabit the area. Somewhere I have a photo of my two hands extended end to end in one of the large bear footprints. The claw marks are clearly visible just beyond my fingers.

When Alvin McGill and Louis Goertzen moved to Smith Inlet, they trapped along the Nekite River. A trapper, who had worked the area before them, never came out. When his body was later discovered, it appeared that a grizzly had ambushed him. It looked like he had been struck down while passing a large stump—he probably never knew what hit him.

I remember another man who was brought to the Port Hardy hospital after a ferocious attack. Something he said struck me as being very funny. One of the nurses asked him what he had been thinking as he was being ripped and torn apart. He replied, "I was thinking—this is a helluva way to die!" Of course he lived to tell the story.

Several years ago, a local resident was taking an evening stroll to check on a secret garden plot in the woods. He wasn't paying attention until his dog gave a warning growl. He looked up to see a bear coming at him but the dog took the bear on and the diversion gave him time to beat a hasty retreat. While running down the narrow trail as fast as he could go, he felt the dog brush past him and then the bear did the same.

He skidded to a stop and it was just like the cartoons. The bear suddenly realized that the man might be easier to target and it skidded on all fours and with feet flailing, it turned to chase the terrified man in the opposite direction. The bear quickly caught up to him and he could only find one small tree to duck behind.

The bear stood almost as high as the tree and it flailed at the man as he dodged blows and watched the branches fly. Then the bear suddenly reached out and clamped him to the trunk before knocking him to the ground. The bear was on top of him when the dog returned and bit bruin in the rump.

Then it was down the trail again. This time he made it to his truck and he admitted later, he was so frightened that he took off and left his dog. The dog found his way home and other than being winded, was none the worse for wear. The man had only one gash to the side of his face. I didn't hear what happened to the garden.

I once hiked to a beaver pond and saw a mother black bear and her cub eating grass beside the water. I watched until they left the area and then I proceeded to the beaver dam. But the bears had only entered the trees and must have been waiting for me to leave. I suddenly heard the cub scrambling up a tree and then the mother came towards me with her head low and swaying and she was huffing and snapping her teeth.

As I slowly backed away, she suddenly jumped a stream that separated us. I had no idea that bears could jump like that and she didn't even take a run at it. Fortunately, when I retreated sufficiently, she returned to her cub.

Another time I saw a most amazing example of a bear's strength and agility. Beside Victoria Lake, a bear ran the wrong way and wound up trapped, on the lower side of the road. Then it climbed a tree but when it was high above the ground, it was exactly at my level and appeared to be much discomforted.

I couldn't help myself; I threw a rock into the branches and the bear actually jumped from the trunk and flew through the air like a squirrel, to land spread-eagle, on the trunk of another tree. This took place high above the ground and it was a good-sized bear. I would not have believed it possible if I had not seen it for myself.

Chapter 15

Killer Whales

Would you have had an adrenalin rush if you had been in the little 14-foot boat that got bashed around by an Orca? (I prefer the word, killer whale—it has more pizzazz) It seems that two young fellows were fishing off Port Renfrew and just as they pulled a prize salmon into the boat, a killer whale's jaws snapped shut behind the tail.

It's hard to say who was more surprised but both parties considered the fish to be theirs. The whale spy-hopped momentarily and then gave them the thrill of their lives as it began to knock the boat around. They did what I think I would also have done; they got- er- in- gear and moved out so fast you could hardly see the froth! I can just picture them, airborne off the waves, crashing into the troughs and sheering, as they hang on for dear-life while one of them scans the surrounding water.

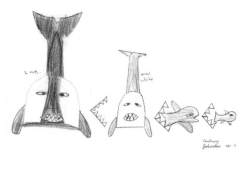

Think about it. These creatures are much bigger than great-white sharks. In fact, they eat sharks, and that includes great-whites. At least the transient whales do because they seem to eat most anything that swims.

As most North Islanders know, the large "resident" pods often seen in Johnstone Straights are fish eaters and they are extremely well educated about commercial fishermen and nets, and thus the homo sapien species in general. In recent years they have been learning about cruise ships, sports fisher people (the few commercial guys and gals left are still fishermen) and tourists.

The transients have been known to attack sea lions, porpoises, and large whales. One tour operator over on the mainland watched gray whales thrash themselves up into the shallows when killer whales were in the area. And another time there had been a massacre of porpoises and one was floating or slowly sinking, just under the surface and beside the boat. Suddenly an orca's head came up from the depths and retrieved the whole creature just as daintily as if it was some little tidbit and the whale never even broke the surface of the water.

I've seen sea lions do similarly. In Ucluelet harbor the sea lions wait for the draggers to come in because they will often drop big dogfish over the side. First, a big dominant bull grabs the whole fish by the tail and with one mighty snap of his neck, the fish cracks the water and splits open, exposing the liver. Then, with a simple slurp, the liver disappears. As the carcass slowly sinks, and if you watch closely, you will see the remainders snapped up in a flash by other sea lions and it all takes place under the surface with barely a ripple to mark the spot. It's really something to see.

Port Hardy resident, Rick Tanaka, was watching whales in Alaska a couple of years ago from his little rubber dinghy. He and his family noticed that whenever they approached the pod the biggest whale always positioned itself between them and the others. As Rick slowly cruised on the surface, he happened to glance down, and there was the large whale coming up from below. Rick was startled and cut the throttle in fear that the whale's head might be nicked by the boat's propeller. Then he backed off but not before his wife was able to snap some good pictures.

Later, an elderly Native man told them that he had once approached the orcas and a whale became very aggressive. When the man tried to speed off the whale became even more excited! It held him against a steep rock wall for a couple of hours and wouldn't let him leave.

Chapter 16

Luna L-98

When my wife asked some newlyweds why they had not enjoyed their honeymoon to the Rockies, the young bride told us that a big animal had kicked her when she tried to pet it. She was very perturbed by the whole episode.

They had come all the way from New York, only to be treated like unwelcome intruders by Canada's wildlife. I smiled but my smile turned to laughter when we arrived at the beautiful town of Banff. We were not at all tempted to closely approach the many large elk, and we did not need the signs to advise us of the foolishness of such activity.

Some time back, CBC television had a feature on Luna the killer whale. Some loony people had been interacting very, very closely with Luna and feeding him. And there was a report that some people had even poured beer down his throat.

Dr. Graham Ellis, of the Pacific Biological Research Station, told me that Luna, known as L-98, was born in 1999. He is a member of the southern resident L pod and became separated from his mother. This is very unusual because he is in good health and growing like a weed.

His mother is still alive but Luna has remained in one location for two years now. He is missing his normal family interaction and comes to humans for company. He has been rubbing against boats and likes to be petted and fed. But this will almost certainly result in disaster for the orca, or some silly people, or both.

"Springer," who was reunited with his family last summer, scared some people badly when he interacted with their boats. But he seemingly reverted to more normal whale behavior when boaters refused to return his interest and affection.

Close interaction is illegal and recently the RCMP laid a charge. Luna will probably reunite with his pod if people will leave him alone. They are advised to speed away, if and when, Luna should approach.

Apart from what people have been feeding him, Luna has been eating wild salmon. And over the winter he has been observed feeding on pilchard.

I asked Dr. Ellis what he thought about interacting with transient orcas and I told him about Dwight Dreger's experience (see True Tale –"Transient Killers"). He chuckled and then said that there are several things to keep in mind.

Transients are very indiscriminate in the types of mammals that they eat. Deer and even grizzly bears are fair game. Thus far, it is theorized that the sonar echo from rubber suits has protected divers from attack. The echo must be different from what the whales are accustomed to.

But there is another danger to also be aware of. Seals and sea lions are so panicked by Transients that they will climb into boats. And remember, these animals are very large. Dr. Ellis has had terrified seals try to climb aboard his vessel.

Several years ago the fishing vessel "Pacific Joye" was returning to Port Hardy from Kitkatla with a load of herring. In Ogden Channel the crew saw a wounded sea lion come streaking to the boat for protection. The poor animal stayed close to the boat and the whales seemed to have disappeared.

For observation purposes the engines were shut down, which made the lion nervous, so it made a run for the beach. All seemed quiet and the men were about to give a cheer, when several dark fins rose out of the water and blocked access to the shore.

Some time later another boat reported the craziest spectacle. A full-grown sea lion was being tossed around like a beach ball by some killer whales. And sadly, the final result was quite predictable. It just came slowly.

I think I wrote the "Luna" story in 2003. Luna died on Friday, March 10, 2006. The little whale lived for seven years and got into trouble for playing too aggressively with boats and float planes. The local Natives claimed he was a chief reincarnated which added spirituality and politics to the saga. He liked the thrust from boat propellers but a very large tugboat proved to be too much for him. He was

38

sucked into the wash and pulverized. It was a very sad day and most (but not all) of the residents of Zeballos and Gold River have greatly missed him.

Chapter 17

Man's Best Friend

If you take a puppy, give him a place to sleep, and a little food, he will be your friend for life. The food can be bare subsistence, and the bed,—a gunnysack under the steps. But for that little consideration he will love you, follow you, obey you and even die for you. It has never ceased to amaze me that a man can curse, kick, and beat his best friend until he cries out in pain and yet that same friend will return with bowed head and tail to plead for just a very little tenderness and appreciation. Whether he gets it or not, a dog will still fight to defend his master even if it means a painful death.

Dogs can talk to people—well, almost. They talk with their tails, eyes and voice. A drooping tail indicates unhappiness or shame; a stiff tail and ruff signals something opposite - disdain, intense concentration, or possible danger. A wagging tail, of course, conveys happiness, and the energy expended is in direct proportion to the pleasure the dog wishes to express. You know how sometimes when someone bothers you, perhaps when you are nearly asleep on the couch (with a warm fire crackling) how you might force a smile? Well, have you ever seen a dog curled up on a rug and nearly asleep, give only one or two weak tail thumps when you tried to engage him in some trivial conversation?

When I was a boy, my dog, Heidi, was sometimes allowed to lie just inside the doorway. But she would use any excuse to wiggle just a little further and a little further into the house. If I talked to her, she would exaggerate her happiness and while thumping her tail vigorously, wiggle closer as she watched carefully for any reaction. If I

39

frowned or cleared my throat in a certain way, she would quickly rush back to her approved spot by the door. Then she would give me that look that said, "You caught me didn't you? Now please don't get excited and put me outside or some such foolish thing. I'll be very, very good and very, very quiet."

When it did come time to put her outside she would plead with deep expressive eyes and unmistakable body language. I still remember her haunting entreaties which went something like this—"How can you put me outside? Can't you see how much I love you? You're just going to shut the door on me?"

Sometimes when it looked to her like my mind was made up she would put her paw on my knee and "whine" asking me to *please* reconsider. If I gave in and said, "Oh, all right," she would thank me over and over again. But if I was firm and insistent she would make me feel just as bad as she possibly could. It helped somewhat if I scratched her ears and explained that she had to go outdoors because she was just a dog. I'm not sure why that helped, but it did.

We sometimes played jokes on each other and she loved a good joke. I could laugh with her but not *at* her or she could be humiliated and deeply hurt. I remember one time in particular. She was adept at catching food thrown to her; I would pretend that I was going to eat the last bite and I would open my mouth slowly, making her savor the taste in her imagination. She would bark or hit me with her paw while her eyes sparkled. I might suddenly throw her a morsel, trying to catch her off guard, but she was always ready and very quick.

Just before bed one evening, I prepared some crackers and shared them with Heidi. She was begging, shaking a paw and sitting pretty etc. while catching cracker after cracker in midair. I had some crackers buttered but I soaked one in soap, craftily reasoning that if I threw it to her, along with the others, she would probably eat it before she caught on.

My trick worked great; she caught and crunched down hard before spitting and gagging. It looked so funny that I laughed uproariously! She was not amused this time. All the sparkle left, and with tail hanging low, she slunk off to bed without saying "Goodnight."

I felt awful and ran after her and threw my arms around her neck, all the while apologizing profusely. She quickly forgave me and licked my face. I convinced her to eat some more good crackers and I promised never, never to humiliate her like that again. And that is a promise I kept.

Dogs' antics often fill precious spots in our memory banks. For example, I have another memory of another dog that came begging to have my daughter throw or "hide" a ball. I held the dog while she searched for a perfect hiding place. I still smile as I remember how she whispered in my ear that she had hidden the ball up on a shelf and she added, "Sh, don't tell Sandy."

In my mind is recorded the scene of a big golden dog rushing excitedly around in circles and sniffing the ground, then the air, finally jumping up as high as possible in order to get a bird's-eye view of the shelf above. Father and little girl stand hand in hand and laugh in disbelief. Some of life's greatest moments are made of just such simple snapshots.

My dog, Heidi, was a beautiful, female, German shepherd and she really was not just my dog but rather a "family" pet. She had been owned by a farmer who wanted us to have her when it became necessary for him to move. Even though we were strangers, she seemed to know that her world had changed and that "we" would now love and take care of her.

She became more my dog because I played with her the most. I was a bird-watcher and often tromped through the woods looking for nests, and she liked to come. This presented a problem because she was anything but quiet! After trying to send her home one day, I just couldn't bear to do it again. It was like whipping someone who loved and adored you. So I took to sneaking out the back door but I only got away with that once. After that she listened intently for the tiniest door squeak and started making regular scent checks around the perimeter of the house just like a true detective.

Heidi was so alert and intelligent looking with her head and tail held high but when friends came to visit, she was embarrassing. With her tail between her legs, she would go and hide. I knew she would not be a good "watch" dog but I was wrong. People told us that when we were gone, they could not get near the place. A little friend of mine said that our dog tore his boot off. He was a wild little guy and I think he was a thief. Heidi always knew when someone was suspicious.

Although she did not know the person asked to come and feed her while we were away, she somehow sensed that this had been arranged and was legitimate. Her previous master told us that she ripped the pants off a man who was trying to steal gas.

It was always fun to come home after a trip because Heidi was so happy to have us back. She was like a little kid, so excited and jumping up and down. She would race around and around the house yipping and yapping. She would roll in the grass and she would try to get someone to chase her. Each day when my brother and I came home from school she would be waiting and watching down the road for us.

Some men like to fish, others like to hunt. Heidi's sport was hunting rabbits but I saw it as a vice, especially after she killed and ate a mother rabbit and all the little babies. But she didn't understand why I was angry or why I whipped her. I decided I loved my dog too much to go through the pain of breaking her of her horrible addiction.

Very rarely did a rabbit get away from her when she spotted it. She could run faster than a rabbit and when her nose was on a hot scent there was almost no chance of escape. If the rabbit found a hole she would dig it out. I once saw her chase two rabbits and catch one; she ate it while still chasing the other and unfortunately, its fate was just as sad. The only good thing about her vice was that while she was off on an assassination mission, I had a few moments to study some birds or look for nests.

Cats were considered fair game also. She chased and killed them if she could but they usually made it up a tree first. I was understandably worried when we brought two kittens home to live with us. Amazingly, they were able to crawl all over her and raised families of their own—all without a speck of trouble, and we didn't have to explain a thing.

Heidi usually chased all dogs off our property and, in fact, killed one once. We found it, deader than a doornail, on its back, with all four legs pointing to the sky. I had to tell the farmer who owned it, what had happened. Tears welled up in my eyes when I saw his sadness. That dog had been his joy and was his connection to his wife who had passed away. He drove to our house and I helped throw his dead friend into the back of his truck.

Heidi didn't understand why I spanked her. Although I said earlier that dogs can almost talk—that *almost* does leave a few gaps. She was confused and I was confused. I realized that she was only protecting our home and doing what she thought we would appreciate. I was unable to explain about the farmer and his love for his wife and why his dog had been the final connection to her life. Heidi let it go just like dogs have been doing for thousands of years. She still adored me as I did her; life went on.

One day male dogs began showing up from near and far and she wasn't chasing them away. My mom said that we needed to lock Heidi in the barn for awhile because we didn't want puppies. I think she meant that "she" didn't want puppies because we kids thought it was a great idea.

Heidi loved to play hide and seek. Someone would hide and when the signal was given, the search would begin. She never gave up and she always got her man—there were no exceptions. Another favorite game was "fetch." She would bring a stick, a ball or a stone, usually to me, because I liked the game almost as much as she did. She always found the correct item and would not return until she did. I suppose that was because if she had the wrong item, I refused to throw it again. When I wanted a break, I would find a stone and throw it into a pond. Sometimes she would search for hours. I would tease and taunt her, telling her to "hurry up!" She would poke her nose under the water and snort furiously. The amazing thing is that she would eventually find the rock and it would be the right one too. As a boy, I figured that she must be able to smell under the water.

One of her favorite games was tug-of-war, the object being, of course, to wrest away from the other protagonist, the stick, rope, or article of clothing. She would growl and I would growl, pretending to be very angry. I would shake her head up and down, twist her until she had to roll, or even twirl around and around like a merry-go-round, with her whole body airborne. The result was always the same—I was the one who got dizzy and sick!

I remember my bones and muscles being jarred and sore from all the furious jerking. About the only way I could win was when Heidi would need to get a better grip and I would quickly yank the item free from her teeth. Then I would laugh and hoot and she would bark. Sometimes I slowly offered her the item only to snatch it back before she could grab it. It was all part of the spoils of victory and we both loved it. When she won, she did exactly to me as I had done to her— she laughed—with her eyes, her tail, her body, her gleeful snort. She couldn't bark with something in her mouth but she could give her victory growl. When I pretended to be very upset, she fairly danced with delight.

Sometimes I would pretend that I was going to sneak the stick or ball while she was sleeping. I would move so slowly and she would seem not to see me but at the last moment she would suddenly snatch the object just ahead of me. And then she would laugh again. Do you think that dogs don't laugh? They most certainly do, at least Heidi did.

One day my dad informed us that we were moving from our country home, with its trees and meadows, to a remote inlet on the British Columbia coast—Smith Inlet, to be exact. We were to live in a logging community where the houses were built on large, log "floats" allowing them to be moved by boat from one ocean setting to another. From our doorsteps we could fish or dive into the water.

My excitement was dashed, however, when I learned that the camp did not allow dogs. My mother did her best to persuade my father and the higher authorities but there was no bending. She was later upset when we found that some of the other people did have dogs. We made arrangements for a school friend to take Heidi as his new pet. Heidi sensed that something was wrong but she did not know quite what. She didn't understand why I was so sad or why all her comforting failed to cheer me up.

The day we said goodbye was a very bad day. Heidi did not usually go for car rides, so she knew that her world was about to flip-flop once again, and the gloomy atmosphere could be felt. She crouched apprehensively, while looking to me for some sign of reassurance. We dropped her off at her new home.

My throat ached; I tried to hold the tears in check but couldn't, when, as we drove away, she made a feeble struggle to get back in the car. She knew it was useless, and as I watched, she gave one last sad gaze and then turned to look up at her new master. I understood, and so did she, that both our worlds had changed forever and there was not a thing that either of us could do about it.

I learned later that she adapted very well and her new owner loved her just as much as I had. She died when a man who did not like dogs, poisoned her. I was saddened and Heidi's little master and friend was heartbroken. It's all a part of growing up.

There is good reason for the dog having become known as man's best friend. Like others of her kind, Heidi's love was limitless and without conditions. My life was enriched, and in my bank of memories, she holds a cherished niche.

Chapter 18

Midnight Snarl

Many years ago my wife and I took our kids and some of their friends to Huston Lake. After supper, we told stories around the campfire and then just before bed someone asked if there was any possibility of cougars lurking about.

I was in the midst of reassuring everybody when I remembered the mountainous terrain on the other side of the lake. Knowing that the hills would probably return an echo, I told my little audience that any cougars would certainly return a cougar yell.

To prove that there were no cougars, I screamed a maniacal, wild, blood-curdling howl (cougars scream like a wild woman, right?) In a few moments, a distant scream returned from across Huston Lake and little eyes widened with fright.

In due time I explained what was really going on and we all experimented with our individual echoes but I was unable to completely alleviate the concerns. My wife was upset with me for scaring everybody and she started hearing things too. In fact, she and the kids were so convinced that they even made me nervous.

That was long ago. More recently my wife and I went camping at the back of Victoria Lake. We saw band-tailed pigeons, flickers, baby grouse, two tiny fawns and a bear. I fished a bit and we thoroughly enjoyed the evening sounds.

Earlier, I had watched a dipper walk on the bottom of a mountain stream. As daylight vanished, blue grouse hooted mournfully, sounding like ghosts puffing on the tops of empty pop bottles. And ruffed grouse drummed in the distance. Swifts could be heard twittering in the sky above us.

The song sparrows and robins went quiet first, - then the thrushes. As a half-moon rose in the night sky, a little owl began to whistle. Strangely, a grouse drummed periodically throughout the night.

I had vetoed my wife's suggestion that we sleep under the stars, because the bugs were really bad. And I reminded her that we were in very wild country. Even a "thin-walled" tent separated us from the outside world, somewhat. That thin layer could also give some advance warning of an attack.

I climbed under the covers, fully clothed, but decided to undress when I became too warm. I had been sleeping soundly, for some time, when Linda shook me awake and I could hear alarm in her voice. She said that a cat had awakened her. "Just out there," she continued. "Shine your light; you'll probably see it."

"A big cat or a little cat," I asked? "I don't know," she replied incredulously, "a big cat." She didn't know why I was asking and I didn't want to alarm her. I was hoping that she was mistaken—maybe she had heard a bird. "Well, what did it sound like," I probed? She replied with a little irritation, "a cat."

46

Midnight Snarl

The truck was some distance away and I hadn't heard the sound, so we zipped up all the flaps—I didn't want any wild animals able to gaze through the thin mosquito netting at us. I checked my watch - 12:15; it would be awhile until daylight. My thoughts turned to cougar attacks in our area; several had been fairly recent and I remembered that one cougar had tried to break through a plastic tent.

The moon had disappeared behind the peaks and it was very dark. Except for the quiet gurgling of a little stream, the outside world seemed to have finally gone silent. I listened intently for awhile and then started to drift off, albeit, somewhat uneasily. I could not forget Dave Parker's brush with death. He lived not far from us and had undergone reconstructive surgery, after barely being able to stab a 100 pound cougar to death.

About thirty minutes later, just outside the tent, there was a mesmerizing, horrific snarl that started with a high pitch and ended with a low, rolling growl. But the word that best describes the feeling was this—paralyzing; the sound was paralyzing! At the same time there was a rush of adrenalin to strengthen my trembling.

Instantly, I cupped my hands to the wall of the tent and gave a yell that should have wakened the dead, but was designed to scare cougars. I did not warn Linda, as I felt that time was of the essence, which is why she would later say that the yell had scared her more than the snarl had.

"Is that the sound you heard," I asked? "Yes," she said, "I tried to tell you." I told her that this was serious and that we were in great danger. I gave her a quick lesson on how to use the pepper spray and told her not to panic and discharge the spray in the tent or on ourselves. It had to be in the face and eyes of the cougar. Then I released the safety button.

We put our clothes on because we felt so vulnerable undressed. Linda took the pepper spray and I took the hunting knife and flashlight. I shone everywhere, including behind us, as we made our way to the nearest door of the truck, where we spent the remainder of the night reclining uncomfortably, in the front seats.

I had been petrified that if the lion was to grab Linda, in the dark, I would never be able to find her. That is why I pushed her in the same door that I also entered. Later, she said, "If only we had the blankets and pillows...." I like to remind her of how I proved my great love and gallantry.

After starting the truck and moving it closer to the tent, and honking the horn, I opened the door. I left the headlights on and extracted a promise from her, that should anything happen, she would come to my aid. She may have told me not to go; I don't remember that part, but at great risk, the blankets and pillows were retrieved.

The next morning was absolutely gorgeous. I suggested that perhaps we should launch the canoe before going home but Linda would have none of it. I wisely decided that it would be the better part of wisdom to throw everything in the back of the truck—pronto.

As I finished writing this story, I asked my wife if I should tell readers about our special spot. She said that she wasn't sure it was our spot anymore. I knew what she meant—leave the place for Lawrence Woodall (Lawrence is an outdoors columnist in the Gazette). We don't go camping for the thrill. We go for the joy. And we are wondering now about the joy.

For some cougar stories in our area, just go to an internet search engine and type (cougar attacks Port Hardy) or something similar.

Chapter 19

Misunderstandings

My father-in-law sometimes uses the wrong words to explain himself and although he now lives in Idaho, we tease him about his heritage from the Ozarks, in Arkansas.

One day he and his brother, Art, installed a water system for a distinguished neighbor lady. Later, when Art was absent, Harold told the lady about his brother's newest hobby. Art had taken up photography, he told her, and even developed his own photos. He told her it had been a secret obsession from boyhood.

To Harold's surprise, she looked displeased and retorted, "He should take pictures of trees!" Harold thought about her strange reaction all afternoon. He knew he had used the word "obsession" and he thought he had used the word "photography." Had he mispronounced something, he wondered?

At home, that evening, Harold shared the woman's strange reaction when he had simply told her about Art's secret obsession with pornography. "No, no, no!" his wife screamed, "Photography! Photography! Photography!"

When I was a young lad, I remember reading a joke in "Reader's Digest" about a gun-slinging cowboy and his son. The boy pointed through a shop window to a brassier and asked his father for an explanation. "Well son," the father drawled, "they're sort of like holsters."

I had heard the term "bra" but not brassiere, and I didn't get the joke so I hollered to the kitchen for help from my mother. I still remember her exact words. She said to my father, "Explain to your son what a brassiere is." And he, knowing nothing of the reason for my question, replied, "Well son, they're something little girls wear to make them look like big girls."

A person has to be careful when asking questions. I take comfort from a story that my wife tells. She was in a biology class and didn't usually speak up. But she was having a good day and decided to ask a question about a term that puzzled her.

She was from the farm and her family didn't use scientific terminology to describe their animals. So she asked the professor what an anus was and she mispronounced the word. When the laughter subsided, the professor told her to ask her lab partner for the explanation. And her male partner told her to please not ask any more questions.

I remember a little boy who was telling me all about his first day at school. "Is your teacher smart?" I asked. He started to nod his head but then stopped. "No," he said. "She doesn't even know how to spell." Apparently he had come to that conclusion when she asked him if he knew how to spell the words "cat" and "dog."

The same little fellow often engaged me in deep conversation. He explained to me one day that the world was in bad trouble due to the state of its deteriorating environment. And he informed me that in our immediate neighborhood he had discovered a polluted pond.

Intrigued, I asked him how he knew. "You could see the pollution," he said. "In fact it was swimming around." The next day he brought me proof. He produced a pop bottle dredged from the mud of a local pond, but there was worse. The real pollution was in a pail of water taken from the same pond.

And when I peered into the murky water I really did see things swimming around. We both gazed upon three very active, wriggling, little tadpoles.

Chapter 20

Mr. Blue

According to the maps, we lived halfway up the British Columbia coast, at the head of an indentation from the ocean. My mother, however, wasted no time with descriptions of Smith Inlet. She simply stated that our home was way out in the sticks.

I was about 13 years old and my father was employed at a small logging camp, built in the old-fashioned coastal style. Our house was part of a series of houses, built on large rafts (floats). Cedar logs were lashed together to make the rafts and the whole floating camp was attached to the beach with long logs called "stiff-legs." These logs held the floats away from the shore when the tide went out. Our yards were the planked enclosures around the houses. You could walk off the floats and step into forty feet of ice-cold water. Any children, who could not swim, wore life belts.

One day, just before school, a large stork-like bird called a great blue heron, was fishing off the edge of the school float. I think it was my cousin, Dennis McGill, who caught a little shiner perch and threw it out on the float where it wiggled and flopped. The heron excitedly flew over and stabbed at the boards with his long beak until he finally picked the fish up and swallowed it. I called him Mr. Blue, and the name stuck.

At recess time, all the kids fished, while Mr. Blue waited nearby. Soon he became very used to us and felt comfortable and safe in our presence. He would wait for recess, noon, and after-school, until someone would come and fish for him. While class was in session one day, he walked along the length of the windows, peering in at us, and only his head showed above the windowsill. Class was disrupted of course, but even the teacher had a good laugh.

Another time, we threw a flounder to Mr. Blue that was much too big to swallow, but he tried and tried anyway. Then he just held it in his bill for a very long time until he finally walked purposefully to the edge of the float and dropped it in the water.

Mr. Blue started following me around, probably because I caught the most fish for him. I would fish from the floats and from a little boat as Mr. Blue watched closely. I would take my fishing line and walk down the series of floats with Mr. Blue right behind. If I stopped suddenly, he would bump into me. If I ran, he would run too. We must have been a hilarious, awkward-looking sight. Once I wanted to see how fast he could run, so I sprinted as fast as I could go. When I checked over my shoulder, panting and heaving, there was Mr. Blue, flying effortlessly along beside me, and looking at me curiously.

I remember once while we were waiting for a fish to bite, Mr. Blue folded up and lay down at my feet. I didn't even know that these birds *could* lie down. I thought they always rested, and even slept, while standing. I thought maybe he was sick but when I caught a fish, he came to life.

Mr. Blue could always tell when I had a fish. He would see the line jerking, and he would shift from foot to foot and peer into the water. He could see the fish long before I could and would often literally dive into the water to try and catch it. I was frightened that he would one day catch my fish, hook and all. Once he did, but I was able to get the fish away from him before he swallowed it. I would sometimes push him, so that I could get the fish and hook first.

The seagulls noticed that Mr. Blue led a pretty easy life and they wanted in on the action. This irritated him to no end, and he would peck at them and chase them away. The camp dogs became used to him and paid him very little attention.

Mr. Blue could be a real glutton and when he ate too much, he would hunker down like a cormorant and look miserable. One day some visitors came to see us and Mr. Blue did all his usual tricks— stabbing at the air to get a fish I gingerly held, diving between my legs etc. I kept live fish in a floating, covered box, and one of the visitors wanted to see what would happen if Mr. Blue had full access to all those fish. So I removed the cover, and Mr. Blue promptly forgot that we and the rest of the world existed.

He ate and ate and ate some more. Then he began to bob; his long neck stretched down, but he couldn't do it. He eventually picked up a fish, and dropped it, but he just couldn't drag himself away from the box. Everyone roared with laughter.

Then someone said, "Make him fly, I bet he's too heavy." I shooed Mr. Blue off his log; he spread his wings and pushed off with his long legs, but he did not get airborne. He fell into the water, and paddled and flapped his way to a rock. Then he hunkered up and looked positively miserable. I was not able to give him an alka-seltzer.

Mr. Blue would not eat bread. And he would not eat meat, but he *would* eat anything fishy. I cut *large* fish into strips, and he swallowed them with relish.

It was amazing to see that long skinny neck stretch and bulge and wiggle as large fish made their last journey down into his stomach. Then he would dabble his beak in the water, give his feathers a shake, and get ready for the next one.

I had to be very careful when handling some of the *spiny* and *prickly* fish, or I could get stabbed and bloodied. Mr. Blue worried not at all. Every fish was flipped until it could be swallowed headfirst. There were no exceptions to that rule. The spines went down better that way.

Often, when the big bird was nowhere to be seen, we kids would wave our arms and shout "Mr. Blue, Mr. Blue." If he was anywhere within seeing distance, he would fly excitedly down to us and skid to a stop. Sometimes, he crash-landed. Once, I was with my family in a rowboat when a heron flew over, high above. We wondered if it might be Mr. Blue, so I shouted, "Mr. Blue, Mr. Blue." The heron went into an immediate dive and swooped down to our head level like he wanted to land in the boat with us. But there was no room for him.

Herons may *look* gangly and awkward, but they are very alert and can become airborne in an instant. I watched eagles try to catch

53

Mr. Blue and his friends, but it was no contest. He and his friends could perform unbelievable acrobatics with twists and turns and somersaults, all the while squawking as if in fun. Eagles do catch herons, but not very often. However, as I was to find out, there is a deadly and silent hunter of herons.

An Imperial Oil tanker delivered our fuel to us. The men laughed about the "stork" up on the house and said something about a baby coming. Mr. Blue did his tricks, and we kids were thrown a carton of ice cream and a package of cookies. So Mr. Blue was starting to be valuable to us.

I have always been amazed with the patience that herons show when hunting on their own. And when that long neck bends, and the bill strikes, there are few misses. I saw Mr. Blue catch long snake-like eels that I never knew existed. When I searched for them, I could only find little tiny eels among the rocks. Herons will eat about any kind of fish, tiny tadpoles, frogs, and even mice.

If you come upon a heron unawares, and it jumps up with that loud hoarse shriek, you can practically be "scared to death" so to speak. And that is the intent, I think. Mr. Blue had several different sounds and tones; sometimes it meant another heron had been sighted, but mostly I didn't know the language. However, there was one early morning when something was very definitely wrong.

Mr. Blue was standing on the roof of the electrical "power-house," and he was emitting a long drawn-out and haunting shriek that seemed not to stop. His neck was stretched full length and he was mesmerized by something that was taking place on the distant shore across the inlet. I could see and hear some excited gull and crow activity, so I took a little rowboat and went to investigate.

I arrived at a crime scene, and no wonder the gulls were so upset! A large and beautiful great-horned owl had killed one of their own, and would not retreat, even when I arrived on the scene.

I had read books by naturalist Sam Campbell, books written for kids and families which I expect should still be interesting for kids today, that is, if they could put "Harry Potter" aside for awhile. I remembered with some worry, that Mr. Campbell had written that these owls were herons' worst enemies. They hunt at night. Their feathers are so constructed as to give soundless flight. And they are powerful, deadly, and efficient killers.

Then one sad morning, Mr. Blue did not show up. All our calling and waving of our arms produced nothing. There was no familiar croak, no crash landing. Later in the day, his half eaten remains were discovered behind the camp, and then we spotted the killer, watching from a tree. We kids caught the owl, but that's another story.

Because Mr. Blue had been such an interesting pet and valued friend, we kids had a funeral service. And somewhere on a hill in Smith Inlet lies Mr. Blue, now reduced to the elements of this earth. I expect that the grave marker has probably rotted away too, so just the memories remain.

Chapter 21

The Silent Killer

A great-horned owl killed our pet heron. When we discovered the half eaten "Mr. Blue," the murderer was watching us from a nearby tree. We gathered up the remains, and then someone had a brain wave.

It so happened that one of the bunkhouse guys had been target-shooting the day before and there was a dead seagull still floating in the water behind our logging camp. It was suggested that we get the gull, throw it to the owl, and then sneak up with gunnysacks.

Lo and behold, it worked! We threw the bait; the owl dropped on the gull and dug its talons in. We kids nervously snuck up, threw the bags over the big owl, and we had him. We stuffed him in an apple box for the time being.

Ken Knopp was pretty handy and he got his dad's tools and all of us kids soon had a big cage constructed, complete with wire mesh and even a perch.

Amazingly, the owl seemed reasonably unconcerned with us and was soon dining on seagull. We watched the feather plucking and the ripping and tearing of flesh. Later, he bobbed his head up and down and gave sort of a triple hoot - the kind of sound one expects to hear only in the quiet of the night.

But when a dog came over to investigate, everything changed in an instant. With its bill clicking, the owl puffed itself up, hissed, and attacked the dog with talons outstretched. Only the screen prevented a violent encounter. Of course, all this was very exciting for us, and we even temporarily forgot about the death of our good friend, Mr. Blue.

After the seagull, the owl ate fish. But we humans have a morbid fascination with power, and killing efficiency, and death. I suppose that is why one little fellow wondered what would happen if a *live* seagull was put in the cage. We all wondered, and the girls were curious too.

Normally, I hated senseless killing. Hunting for meat was one thing, but I hated to see some of the guys shooting even seagulls and crows for no reason. Something told me this live-seagull-thing was not a good idea, but I too was fascinated with the thought.

Isn't it interesting that *no* adults and especially no *female* adults were consulted as to the morality and ethics that could possibly be involved in the gathering of food for our new mascot? A couple of fellows in the lower grades put out some bread pieces inside a string with a pull-noose. Before long, a gull was in hand. Warning: The following subject matter may not be suitable for all readers.

I've always been fascinated with wild creatures' response to danger. In this case, the poor little seagull knew he was facing death in the face. It silently and quickly checked every corner of the cage while the owl watched. School kids watched too; in fact, there was hardly room to see.

Suddenly, the owl dropped, and grabbed the gull's neck with its talons. There was no cry, and no struggle. It was almost as if the gull knew all along that this was how it would end. And this type of feeding ended too—immediately, post haste—as soon as the mothers got wind of what had taken place.

I don't remember exactly how long we imprisoned the silent death machine, but eventually one of the men let the owl go without even consulting us. And so ended the Saga of Mr. Blue and the Silent Killer.

Chapter 22

Night of Terror

The "North Island Gazette" of September 26, 1974, carried the story of my father's capsize in Seymour Narrows, British Columbia. And as commentator Paul Harvey would say, "Here's the *rest* of the story."

My father, Roy McGill, cannot tell his story anymore because in April of 1997 he suffered a debilitating stroke, which took him to the point where he now needs total care. Thankfully, I suppose, Roy's present mental state is such that he seems not to understand the full seriousness of his condition. But sometimes when his eyes show lack of recognition or emotion, the recounting of this story—*his* story—snaps him back to some sense of reality and belonging.*

My dad worked for the Port Hardy municipality for a time and a fellow employee needed someone to take his fish boat to Campbell River. My father (Roy) became that person. He didn't mind, because years earlier, he had owned his own boat and sort of relished the opportunity to take a quiet cruise down Johnston Straights to Campbell River—about 14 hours by boat.

It is important to pass through Seymour Narrows at "slack tide" (a short period of time before the current switches directions). Daylight had long vanished when Roy reached this trouble spot and it was here that his engine coughed and quit.

After a quick assessment Roy decided that he needed some fuel and the lights on shore led him to believe that there might be a fuel station nearby. He was never one to ask for help or ask for directions or anything of the sort if there was any possible way on earth that he could take care of himself. He just wanted enough emergency fuel to get the boat to the nearest harbor.

He reasoned that if he hurried he should be able to row the boat's dinghy to shore and back before the current became too vicious. The larger vessel appeared to be circling quietly in a back-eddy. But in the darkness he misjudged the current and close to shore the dinghy suddenly flipped.

The date was September 15, 1974; the night was fully developed, and the upwelling water was frightfully cold. Worse, was the fact that whirlpools were developing and not a soul knew of his predicament.

As he was carried along he could hear the sounds of splashing waves and the ominous sucking of whirlpools. Then he was in one. His eardrums hurt and his lungs nearly burst before he could get to the surface. The dinghy was his only floatation and he refused to let it go as he spun downwards.

When the funnel narrowed, somewhere in the depths, he kicked out of it and frantically clawed for the air above. But after one frantic gasp, water washed over his head as he was bashed from all sides by current slop. He grabbed air when he could but then another whirlpool took him under. Relief was followed by despair as this scenario repeated itself over and over.

Weeks later he would suffer terrible nightmares and wake in sweat as the awful memories continued to plague him. Flashbacks included memories of the bowline that extended longer than the skiff. As he twirled down into the blackness, the rope wrapped around his legs. His dreams were haunted by the memory of his panic.

Then came the numbing cold; my dad could feel the beginning of the end. To keep his circulation going, he literally beat every part of his body against the skiff. There apparently was a period of time, after the whirlpools, when warmth was his greatest concern.

At some point, traffic passed him. Two tugs with tows went by and he thought one might even run him over. A searchlight was turned full force in his eyes, and with relief, he waved frantically. But the tug carried on. This, he said, was his most discouraging moment.

My dad was 56 years old and had spent most of his life in the mill and logging industries. He was a healthy, powerful man and a teetotaler and vegetarian. But I'm not sure that his health was ever as robust after this experience. I'll never forget the dark line that crossed each fingernail, evidently caused by his desperate grip on the dinghy. Eventually that reminder of his ordeal grew out and disappeared when his nails were trimmed.

Dad was a man of faith, even though for the most part, he practiced his beliefs quietly. He often told me, especially after he lost his wife, that God had been so good to him. As far as I know he did not attempt to answer the questions concerning why we sometimes live and why we sometimes suffer and die.

Strangely enough, dad did not seriously consider the possibility of dying until the third and final tug came into view. He knew that he could not survive the rapids again when the tidal current switched directions. He told the Lord, "If this is my time to die, I'm ready, but if I am to be rescued, it has to be now."

When the tug was as close as it would get, Roy used his final energy to give his woodsman's yell. Instantly a voice answered, "Yes, I hear you!" the sweetest words ever uttered.

I've often wondered how that man could hear above the noise of water and engines. Was he on deck, and if so, why? (I've tried to follow up, but was unsuccessful).

Immediately upon rescue, dad went into painful spasms and muscle cramps. The tug's crew massaged his muscles and gave him rum to drink. The next morning he called from Campbell River and told my mother to come and pick him up at the hospital. Then he hung up. He didn't say *which* hospital and he didn't explain why he was there. Maybe it was the rum.

Names are interesting. His problem boat—"Lone Eagle." The rescue boat—"Storm King."

I'm told that normal survival time would be 15-45 minutes. Roy survived 40-degree water for three hours until his rescue about one a.m. in the morning. The Narrow's whirls and chilling cold didn't get him. There are not many who could duplicate that feat. Certainly, there's no one who would want to try.

This story was written after his stroke but before his death. Roy McGill passed away in July of 2002.

Chapter 23

Otscar

Many years ago, Dennis McGill and I decided to build a natural outdoor aquarium. We lived on a floating log camp and one day, after school, we sunk a large shipping crate in the water. After attaching circulation screens, we added sand, rocks, and kelp.

Then we caught crabs, prawn, herring, flounders, kelp cod, perch and rock cod for starters. We added other more exotic species too, like eels, but we found that our captives did not like the food we gave them. They began to eat each other; it was very frustrating.

The herring (or maybe they were anchovies) would not eat anything. But I noticed that they ate little shrimp creatures and worms in the wild, so I peeled the thread-like edge from a mussel. It looked like a little worm in the water and the fish snapped it up. I was quite proud of myself for having tricked them, or so I thought.

I had read a strange story in one of Sam Campbell's books about a wild fish that came when its name was called. This pike would jump in excitement as it anticipated a treat. I decided to experiment.

"George" was a kelp cod (greenling). I would call his name and up he would come from the bottom. I fed him the soft innards of crushed mussels and he nibbled at my fingers. I experimented in different ways and he always came rushing to meet me. But I wonder, now, if my experiment was really performed in a "scientific" manner.

Perhaps George heard vibrations. Even though I tried to tiptoe, perhaps he felt my walking. Maybe he actually saw me, although I thought I had ruled that out at the time. Maybe a fish farmer can settle this question.

One day Dennis excitedly told me that there was a creature in the aquarium. I rushed out to see but visibility was impossible because the water was all stirred up with mud. Suddenly, an otter popped up, and we jumped, and it jumped, over the side of the aquarium. George was never seen again.

Now we had a new plan. Instead of an aquarium, we would have an otter pond. We restocked with any kind of fish we could catch and the otter obliged us by eating them. But we couldn't keep up; it became work.

One day, when I should have been doing my school correspondence, I saw the otter checking the aquarium, which was empty. I had a fish saved and I carefully splashed it back and forth in the water. The otter stretched its neck and coughed and snorted before slipping under the surface.

I had no idea what it would do next so I very gingerly held the fish half in, and half out, of the water. I did not see the otter but suddenly the fish was yanked from my hand. As otters are master "escape" and "sneak" artists, it must have swum along a log before darting out to grab my fish.

Then I flapped a fish up and down against the boards where I stood, and offered it when the otter came closer. Soon it had no fear and was taking fish from my hand.

Oscar was the name of a famous seal, so Oscar with a T seemed appropriate for an otter. Otscar became our camp mascot but one morning my mother called me to say that the otter should have been named Otscarina. I didn't understand, so she said to come with her and

I would see why the name was wrong. I couldn't help but laugh when I saw the little kits she had in tow, but she had been "Otscar" for too long; the name stuck.

The little otters had a high-pitched whistle, or trill that sounded like a bird. The adults whistled too, and snorted and grunted often, in some kind of otter talk. When the otters dove under the water, they left a bubble trail that showed where they had gone.

Otscar knew that we would not hurt her babies but she became very protective and aggressive when the camp dogs came around. Previously, the otters had loved to tease the dogs. They would pop up just out of reach, in the water, and puff and snort at the dogs and drive them wild. Other times they would entice a dog onto a log and while one otter kept its attention from the front, another would come from behind. The dogs hated the otters.

I saw Otscar come right out of the water to chase one of the large dogs until they were baring teeth nose to nose. The dog seemed to know that this was deadly serious and dangerous, so it dared not attack.

I heard a trapper say that an otter had once got hold of his boot and bit right through the steel toe. I know that they could crunch up any fish with all the bones in very short order. And once when I stuck the tail of a fish through a crack in the planks, the otters ripped big chunks of wood off with their teeth.

Otscar sniffed my boot one day and then grabbed it with my toes still inside, giving me the scare of my life! I yanked my foot away and frightened Otscar but she soon came back. I realized that she was only mouthing my foot much the way a dog does when playing with its master.

We gave Otscar a three-foot, live, wolf eel one day and she ate the poor sea creature from the tail end, while holding it down. I read a report recently that says fish do not actually feel pain—I hope it's true.

I was curious to see just how large a fish could be handled by Otscar, so I loosely tied a string through the gill cover of a monster, toothy, ling cod and threw it into the otter pond (old aquarium crate). It was a terrible fight but the otter came up with the fish that was longer than she was, and there was some great feasting.

Our otter loved to play tug-o-war. We would tie a fish on a string and throw it out into the water. Otscar would dive from the wharf and try to "catch" the fish before we retrieved it. If we won she would wait for us to throw the fish again; it was great fun for all concerned. In the winter, she liked to chase snowballs too.

When Otscar caught the fish, there was a lot of splashing and tugging, but she quickly learned that if she could make it under the logs and brace herself, she would always win the contest.

It was so much fun to see the otter streak through the water. Otters swim like porpoises, with the whole body flexing in unbelievable grace and speed. Their feet are webbed, but they do not dog paddle. Rather, they extend their back feet for sort of a flat, tail-like effect. The front feet are tucked alongside when swimming, but are used for steering, quick stops and turns.

Otscar refused to eat dog fish (sharks) but she ate any other type of fish and unfortunately, loons, and really enjoyed canned salmon, too. One day, Port Hardy resident, Irene Sheard came to visit. Irene had just cleaned a sockeye salmon, when the otter stole it from her; at least I think that's the way the story goes.

None of Otscar's family or friends ever became quite as trusting as she was. Years later, she was still alive when we moved from Smith Inlet.

Chapter 24

Pal

When I was 8 years old, I lived in a small and close-knit sawmill community. Several families owned dogs, but one little heavy-set dachshund was *everyone's* dog.

He was black and was sometimes affectionately called a mutt, because he had more in him than just dachshund. He loved people and especially enjoyed being with kids. Because he was such a people-oriented dog, he was given the name "Pal", a name that made all visitors smile because it was so appropriate.

One of the sawyers, John Smith, (not his real name) obtained a puppy, which grew into a large black dog of unknown genetic background. This dog had a bad attitude from its earliest days. Maybe it was treated unkindly. At any rate, it minded its owner, but seemed to respect no one else.

While the stinker was small, Pal made him mind his manners, but the little dog grew and Pal had a tougher and tougher time. The day came when poor old Pal got a good licking (of the unpleasant kind) and from that time on his life was made miserable by the other dog. Even though Pal did his best to avoid trouble, the *bully* dog took every opportunity to beat him up. Pal had to grovel and beg for mercy in front of everybody.

One day when Pal was getting a beating, and squealing with pain, some other dogs began attacking him too. As if he didn't have enough trouble already! I could not believe it. The other dogs sided with the bully against poor little Pal who never hurt anybody. I have since discovered that people do very much the same thing. In fact people do it *worse* and probably did it first.

The children were powerless to help Pal. The bigger dog would just "dare" anyone to help. If any of us picked up rocks he would growl and come stiffly right up close. The rocks were always dropped back on the ground.

Pal

We thought of many plans—like squirt guns with bleach—for the mean dog's eyes; bows and arrows, but in the end, nothing worked, mainly because each of us was too frightened to be the leader. Like the story of the mice, *who* was going to put the bell on the cat?

Fate changed the situation entirely, and the balance of power switched to a new dog that moved to the community, along with "Dallas" the dog's owner. Dallas was a little older than me and he told me his dog's name was "Rex."

Rex was a lovely, part German-shepherd dog, very kind, loved kids, and especially loved Dallas. Rex followed Dallas everywhere and Rex got along well with little "Pal", consequently, Pal stuck close.

The bully dog could not boss Rex around. They had some fierce battles—very bruising and bloody affairs! We began to see less and less of the mean dog as he began sticking nearer to home.

One day when school convened, Dallas was missing. We learned that his dog had come home very sick and appeared to be dying. Dallas was heart-broken and couldn't control his tears.

When I went home for lunch that day, my mom told me that there was a mystery afoot. Someone had shot Rex but the dog had made it home to his friends before dying painfully from his wounds. The community was buzzing and the gossip was that Mr. Smith had done the shooting.

Mr. John Smith denied having had anything to do with the unfortunate episode but when some of the men suggested retrieving the bullet, he confessed. He claimed that there had been a terrible fight between his dog and the now deceased pet. He had shot his .22 rifle, he said, without taking aim at either dog—in fact, he had turned his back and simply shot towards them.

The neighbors kept buzzing. Something needed to be done and the sawmill owner did it. Mr. Smith was told that he should shoot his own dog also, or find other employment. A sense of justice might make the atmosphere pleasant once again.

It must have been much harder for Mr. Smith to pull the trigger this time, for he really did love the dog nobody else could love. Peace was eventually restored to the community.

And Pal? He *loved* the world without his former enemy, and lived many happy years.

Chapter 25

Hardy Bay Blockaded

We were halibut fishing somewhere out in the blue between Port Hardy and the Queen Charlotte Islands. There was only water, water, everywhere, with no land in sight, but as far as the eye could see, were hundreds of Pacific white-sided dolphins rolling and jumping on the surface.

I noticed, way off the starboard bow, about twenty dolphins leaping high into the air and in perfect formation, over and over again. But something was not quite right and I couldn't put my finger on what the problem was. So, with my binoculars, I took a closer look and then I saw something absolutely amazing.

Mixed in with the dolphins, were many smaller Fur seals, and they were flying out of the water just as fast and just as high as were their friends. In fact, except for the size difference, I probably wouldn't even have noticed. Here were these very different mammals, playing together way out in the middle of the ocean, and we were privileged to come upon the action.

Although I haven't seen one for a long time, these little seals sometimes get lost while migrating up the coast to Alaska. At these times, some may pop up in Hardy Bay or one of the inlets. They have very little fear and you can sometimes touch them. At our Smith Inlet logging camp, Ernie Knopp once put one by the stove for awhile, and the little animal immediately made himself right at home.

Hardy Bay Blockaded

We live in an area where you do not always have to go far to see nature in action. Port Hardy residents will remember that just a few years ago, tons and tons of pilchards (sardines) began to die in Hardy Bay. These fish are very oily; my seine boat was caked with the horrible grease, and it was an awful mess to clean up.

Over a period of weeks, the gulls moved in to eat the fish as they swam in a fluttering and sickly manner. Then the word got out to the sea lions, and the huge Stellar sea lions showed up along with their smaller California cousins. After that, the transient Killer whales arrived to feast on the sea lions. But did you know that one day the whales blockaded the inner harbor?

I was driving into town along the old scenic route and was surprised to see porpoises leaping in unison, out in front of the Glen Lyon Inn. But I still kick myself for not looking out a little further. My cousin, Lloyd McGill, told me what happened.

The Killer whales had herded the porpoises into the inner basin of the harbor until they were trapped. Then the whales formed a blockade across the bay, out by the fish boats. They watched quietly as the frantic porpoises wore themselves out in panic.

On some sort of a signal, the whales rushed in like killer submarines. There was a lot of splashing and thrashing, and a bloodbath. And I missed it, right in my own back yard.

Most of us have a fascination with these big animals because of their ferocity. Could they present a danger to humans? When I posed that question to an expert, the biologist said, "I would not swim when transients show up."

There have been some mishaps and close calls and tense moments. I will write about some of these next week. And I may tell you about the time, many years ago, that my brother and I thought three Killer whales were going to rip the side right off our little aluminum skiff!

Chapter 26

Transient Killers

My brother and I were just two kids rowing a little boat back to our logging camp. We were about a third of the way across the channel, when we saw three Orcas coming out of the Inlet.

We calculated that our paths would intersect about midway, and because we were unsure of the whales' eating habits, we held a quick conference. After visualizing the boat ripped to pieces and the occupants in the water (and that was before the eating frenzy began) we agreed that it might be the better part of wisdom to return to the shoreline.

The camp was a fair distance away and I hoped no one was watching us. We thought we would play it cool and just get *near* the shore, but the Orcas changed course and came for us (or so we thought). When Gary jumped out of the boat, I decided to do likewise. We climbed up the beach with the bowline in our hands just before the 3 large beasts swam directly under our boat, and in the clear water we could see them checking us out.

When it was safe to return to camp, we met one of the loggers doubled over with laughter, the very thing we had hoped to avoid. He said he had been watching the whole episode with his binoculars. Then he added, "As those *blackfish* got closer, I even saw you get out on the beach." But we felt better when he said that he would have done exactly the same thing.

Bush pilots hear lots of stories and a pilot friend related a story that took place in the same inlet where the previous encounter occurred. Apparently a logger was filming an attack by Orcas, on dolphins, in Security Bay. The man was standing on a wharf and a terrified dolphin jumped right over it. Pursuing the dolphin was an Orca, and the whale actually hit the dock.

Even more exciting was the experience told by a friend who stopped sports fishing, one day, to check out a little rock island at the top of Johnstone Straits. He got out of the boat while his friend held the bowline. Nearby was a seal that was behaving very strangely. Instead of rushing to the water, it just looked at them and refused to move.

Suddenly a killer whale launched itself out of the water and partially slid onto the rocks beside the man holding the boat. He could have touched it and the experience was truly startling and frightening. They eyed each other for a few moments before the large animal slid back into the water.

The experts tell us there have been no attacks on humans, at least not on our coast. But I previously wrote about two sports fishermen who had their boat knocked around a bit. And of course, there was the Victoria whale trainer who was killed by his trainee. Two National Geographic photographers got a thrill when Killer whales tried to break the ice they were standing on (as they do for seals, which they eat). And I read about a diver (not in B.C.) who was backed into a small cave by an Orca. Fortunately, the whale could not reach him, but it did try. The surface crew diverted the whale's attention by forcing some seals into the water.

These stories came rushing to my memory one day in November of 1998, when I looked out to the red blinker in the middle of Hardy Bay. Pilchards (sardines) had attracted the seagulls and sea lions and then the Killer whales had moved in. But I was alarmed on this day, when I noticed that my friend, Dwight Dreger, was diving for urchins out by the light.

Dwight's tender- boat was surrounded by sea lions, acting as if they were insane. I realized why, when I saw some big black dorsal fins break the surface. And then I worried for my friend's safety.

On closer inspection, I realized that the Orcas had caught a sea lion and it was getting a thrashing. As the two big adults circled about, three little killers pummeled and bludgeoned the poor creature. Then one of the big whales submerged and suddenly the water erupted in spray and foam as the sea lion was thrown into the air. The whole spectacle slowly moved towards the Tsulquate Reserve, where Pastor Don Felkley was able to get some video shots from his house.

Dwight later reported that he had backed against a rock wall when about 25 sea lions rushed towards him, as the Orcas excitedly clicked and whistled. And he had thought that they were eating fish...

Chapter 27

Politically Correct

My wife tells me that I must become more sensitive and aware of our society's changing vocabulary. However, she does admit that the term "fisher" is just too corny. But I cannot call Indians, Indian anymore, even though my native friends call themselves Indian all the time. She says that they can, but I can't. Who decided these things?

I really don't care whether I'm called white, Caucasian, European, Scottish, or honkie. The tone of voice has a lot to do with it.

But some terms do have negative connotations. I once told a black employee to wrap a rope on the "capstan" and I pointed, trying to re-member sailboat terminology. "You mean the niggerhead?" he asked. I just shrugged; sometimes you can't win. I still do not like that word, but most fishermen use it innocently, without thinking.

And then there's the term "racist." A fisherman friend had an unknown black man walk up to him and without warning, the man punched him in the face. That black man was extremely prejudiced. Perhaps whites, or even white racists, had mistreated him or his parents, and the evil had rubbed off. And if my friend had stayed in that U.S. environment, he might have become hateful too.

Out of curiosity, I asked my (adopted) Native sister if she had ever been discriminated against or treated differently because of her race.

She replied that she had never noticed or even thought about it. I found that quite interesting because I hear the term thrown about quite freely at times. But the accusations are almost always directed toward the white society, and not the other way around.

I told a non-native person recently, that he would probably be resentful if his parents had once owned a great big farm but had been pushed into a little tiny corner, and had their way of life changed forever. This is a worldwide problem and for thousands of years people have been killing each other over these very kinds of issues.

When Europeans arrived on the west coast, they found Indians fighting each other—the tribal animosity was severe. The southern tribes fought amongst themselves but banded together to fight the Bella Bellas, Haidas and Tsimpshians. Treachery was common; some tribes were nearly wiped out by other tribes, and the healing has come slowly. If boundaries existed, they were not always respected. The men were often killed and the women and children taken as slaves.

Captain Walbran recounts in the book, *British Columbia Coast Names*, that in the summer of 1860, the Cowichans invited some Bella Bellas and a white man to come ashore at Saltspring Island. They then shot the Bella Bella men and took the women and boys as slaves. A few days later, Fort Rupert canoes came by and spied two Cowichans racing for the safety of some white men. But the Cowichans had their heads cut off and their bodies thrown into the water. The whites were spared, although they were frightened to death. No explanations were given but the next day one of the heads was found impaled on a pole.

Locally, the last slave was murdered in the early 1890's, partly as a reaction against European law. The Native man who killed his slave, just wanted to show that he could do it if he wanted to. Not everything about the good old days was good.

Europeans did take advantage, Europeans did mistreat, as all humans have been doing for thousands of years. The short-term solutions are not easy but I believe our world's awful experiment with sin is nearly finished and I do believe that we desperately need the impartial Creator to help us sort things out.

Chapter 28

Rescue At Sea

CARLYE SHEDLEY II

The year was about 1958 and Lloyd McGill must have been 14 years old. He was excited to be gillnetting with his brother, Lance. His age then, and his age now, could affect some of the finer details of this story but this is what he remembers.

The fishermen up and down the coast talked to each other on channel 2318 because that channel, and the Coast Guard channel, was all they had. The big radios reached all over the coast and the VHF radios with their multitude of high frequencies were not in use yet.

The big radios had tubes and Lance and Lloyd's father had told them to mostly leave the radio turned off because it drained the battery. One would just have to break in and talk over somebody else to use the working channel. It was a constant, noisy barrage of screaming chatter.

But Lloyd's attention was riveted, one evening, when a worried boy's voice said, "I can't find my dad." Somehow, above all the noise and confusion (it may have been because of his higher pitch) his message came through. Others responded, and ever so slowly, the roar of noise almost miraculously subsided.

The Bull Harbor Coast Guard station monitored that channel and the whole fishing fleet up and down the coast, listened transfixed, as the details of an emergency came forth. An officer told the boy to do another thorough search of the whole boat. He was advised to check the bunks, hatches, bow and stern and to look up on top of the cabin also.

Shortly, the boy's voice said, "I've searched everywhere and I still can't find my dad." The officer then asked the boy if he thought he could steer the boat and operate the controls. The boy responded, "I think so."

The advice was then given to turn the boat around and go back exactly in the opposite direction. The boy was told to follow the foam and bubbles as best possible and to keep a sharp eye peeled.

A long silence followed as the whole coast anxiously awaited developments. Eventually the little voice said, "Yes, I see my dad but he's not moving."

The boy was instructed to carefully get as close as possible and quickly get a rope around his father. Lloyd says that he thinks the boy must have got a line on the man and used the gillnet drum to help haul the body aboard.

After what seemed forever, the fleet listened in horror as the boy reported that he had his dad aboard but he still was not moving. A subtle tone conveyed the sense of futility in the officer's voice as he instructed the boy to roll his father on his stomach and try to drain the water from his lungs. Then he was to roll him back and forth and push on his chest and back vigorously.

The silence on the normally noisy radio was now deafening. Finally the boy's voice said with excitement, "He's breathing. He's alive." A cheer was heard all the way from Vancouver to Prince Rupert in the far north.

Lloyd says that the chatter very gradually began again and increased to a dull roar until the peace was again lost in the din and confusion of work at sea.

Chapter 29

Some Logging Stories

We human beings are a strange bunch. Take working in the woods for instance—if someone gets knocked by a log and killed, we get quiet or sullen or we might even shed some tears, but if it's really close, we laugh and slap our legs as if the biggest joke ever, just took place. Let me give some examples.

Many years ago, Louis Goertzen was standing at the landing with some other guys as a "turn" of logs was coming in by skyline. It was a long haul, using the old spar tree method. Standing there with him was a visitor from the city who knew very little about logging; I guess you would say he was a tourist.

There was some sort of a hang-up and suddenly the steel mainline jerked, and momentarily, hung in waves way up above. Everybody instinctively dove for cover as the line began screaming and whipping down the hill and through the block high overhead. In seconds, it had roared down the hill and coiled with a huge noise and dust cloud all around the tourist. He was looking in bewilderment at the chaos and then realized that he was the only one in sight. So he dove down beside all the line that had somehow missed him, and was coiled on the ground. When everybody else came crawling out of their hiding places, he was still snuggled up against the heavy line that had nearly killed him. And everybody roared with laughter! Why? Because he wasn't dead.

I remember when Alvin McGill was breaking some of us young kids in as choker-men. We were just set to have a rest as some logs were heading in, when a line flew off a stump and a log came sailing through the air about head level. We hit the dirt and tried to find holes under stumps! I will never forget the worried look on Alvin's face as he came up, and then began grinning when he saw the rest of us also pop up one- by- one. We were soon doubled up with laughter as we discussed who had looked the silliest, and who had found the most

74

ridiculous hiding place. Logging was idled for a while as Alvin told us he wished we could move that fast when there was work to be done.

Another time, a mother bear and cub came along and disrupted work and we went out to have a look. Both bears were up a tree and I asked what we would do if they came down. One young fellow said, "No problem." He would just start the power saw that was nearby for fighting hang-ups. He then pulled the saw out from under a stump and was checking it out, but his back was turned. I whispered to the other guys, and on a signal, we all went running past him as if in a panic. We screamed that the bear was coming.

He dropped the saw and didn't even look back to check things out. Then he went running right over my brother with his logging boots— at least that's what we accused him of. He had a hard time living it down.

Louis Goertzen was Alvin's partner. He had these sayings that we heard over and over. He said that he didn't mind work at all; he just didn't like working between meals. And he also said work didn't scare him a bit. He could lay down right beside it and go to sleep.

Often, on the way home after work, he would look at the salmon berries along the road and remark that we probably weren't getting enough vitamin C, since we lived way out in the sticks (Smith Inlet). Most of the other guys just wanted to get home and didn't care about vitamin C. Someone might say that you had to watch out for the worms. And he would usually snort, "Watch out for the worms? They have to watch out for themselves!"

And he had another saying that was so good; I often use it. When a knife was needed to cut or trim something, he would ask, "Who's got a knife?" He was the only one who ever had one, and after gazing at each person and giving sufficient time for silent contemplation, he would say, "A man with a knife is worth 50 cents more an hour."

Louis and Alvin were timber cruising one day and Alvin said, "Look at the bear." Louis was looking all over and couldn't see it. The bear was peaking out of a den hole at his feet. In fact, it couldn't come out because Louis was blocking its path from under a tree. When

Louis looked down, he was so shocked that both he and the bear went running away together.

I was working for "Borer Logging" one summer and it was so hot that no one wanted to work on the steep side-hill. In desperation, Andre talked two truck drivers into giving it a try. The next day only one of the men was able to get out of bed. He said that his friend had phoned him the night before and claimed to have lost 16 pounds. When the other man weighed himself he found that he had lost 18 pounds.

Andre had a nickname for Joe Nelson. He called him Grumpie Joe, or just Grumpie, for short. This one day Joe was hook-tending at the back of a steep hill. A long skinny log got loose above him and increased speed as it slid down the hill. It would sheer as it hit stumps, and sometimes it was airborne. There was no way to tell which direction it would take next. At first Joe just watched it; then he dashed one way and stopped. It was coming for him, so he changed directions. The log changed directions too.

Those of us on the landing down below him, looked up as a terrifying scene developed. Joe ran out of time and options. We watched as he made several short bursts here and there. Then he dove down behind the only available stump and made himself as small as possible. The log made one more turn and then became airborne again, and shivered, before crashing into the very stump Joe was hugging. It sheered and went racing and slipping past the edge of the stump, just inches from Joe.

Howie Cheetam was running the yarder, and when the dust cleared he came out on deck yelling and screaming and holding a rag. He made motions to the effect that if Joe didn't have toilet paper, the rag would do. Joe was not amused; at least not then. He was too busy smoking cigarettes.

Chapter 30

The Birds and the Bees

I remember asking my parents why the cows were rearing up on each other in the springtime. My mother ordered my dad to give an explanation to the question, so he said that some of the cows (bulls) were very lazy and liked to "rest" on the others, sort of piggyback style. I laughed and thought that was as good an explanation as any I could come up with. But I did wonder why my mom gave a funny look and shook her head.

I've always thought that a part of my education was sadly lacking, but my brother says that he remembers mom reading a book to us. He says that he did not believe the explanation of how we came to be; I do not even remember the story. Maybe I was not paying attention.

My mother was a wise woman with years of experience with children. Her advice to my wife and me was to wait for the questions and then to load the little computer minds carefully. "Don't give them too much," she said. She felt that many parents mistakenly give too much information and more than is even desired by the children asking the questions. She said that more detailed explanations should be tailored to age.

My mother said that comparison to a "seed" was very effective in explaining the facts of life. The seed grows within the mother and a little baby is eventually born. At the early stages, she assured us, there were usually no further questions.

She appeared to be right; everything went according to plan with our daughter. Then one day my little boy popped the question and took me by surprise—he was so small. I rambled about life and beginnings and made mention of the seed…

"But," he asked, "How does mommy "get" the seed?" At that point I mumbled just a little and explained that there would be a later explanation. I think I added something about these types of topics remaining within the family circle. He seemed satisfied and trotted off to play, leaving me to ponder the good old-fashioned stork.

When I was small, I thought the doctor simply "gave" my mom and dad a baby, and that was good enough. Later, when I learned about the baby growing in the tummy, that was also satisfactory. Some things just happened.

Many weeks went by. Then one day, like a thunderbolt from the sky, everything came crashing down. It was at church. My boy loudly disagreed with the idea that Jesus had made him. He told his teachers and friends that "*he*" had come from a seed that daddy gave to mommy. Although he had not seen the seed, he really wondered how it tasted. Of course! Why hadn't I thought of that?

Like my mother before me, I bought a book. The kids didn't like it. It was a long time before I tried anything further, and when I did, my kids put their fingers in their ears and said they already knew that stuff. And that's how we covered the facts of life.

Chapter 31

The Green String

I begged my dad for permission to borrow his roll of nylon twine. He was reluctant, because as he carefully explained to me, the string was green and could be easily lost. He finally said, "Okay, but remember, the string is the same color as the grass. Don't lose it. It's the only string I've got."

I grabbed my friends, Bruno and Jackie, and we rode our bikes out into ranch country. Before long, we found a colony of Columbia ground squirrels and watched them scamper into their homes in the ground.

We selected a hole, placed a lasso-type noose around it, and unrolled the twine a sufficient distance to where we could hide behind a bush. We waited impatiently until a head popped up but the squirrel immediately noticed the string and began to nibble at it. My friends whispered several times to pull the string but the squirrel's head wasn't out quite far enough.

Finally he came half way out; I yanked the string and we had him. He pulled like crazy; it was more fun than catching a trout. But our excitement and yelling was short-lived when the string broke. The squirrel's nibbling must have weakened the loop.

We waited and waited but the little creatures waited longer, and we became impatient. So we flipped some "cow pies," gathered worms, and went fishing.

Several hours later, we returned for the string but it wasn't there. It had somehow blended into the grass just as my dad had warned it would. I panicked and flushed. I could just imagine my dad's scornful and piercing look, before he said, "What? Didn't I tell you?"

We fanned out, we went in parallel, we went in circles, and then we gave up. One of my friends said, "Let's pray." It seemed the obvious thing to do and was the only option left.

We were kids. Our faith was strong. We actually believed the Bible stories about God's care for us. We had heard story after story of answered prayer and we had been told that God cared very much for kids and listened to their requests. We had even learned that Jesus had said that adults needed the faith of children.

We knelt in a circle and simply talked to Jesus. I told Him that I really, really needed to find the string because I had made a promise to my dad. When we opened our eyes, the ball of string was within our circle and in easy reach of each of us. We were thrilled, but not particularly surprised. I do not even remember saying Thank you. I did not breathe a word of it to my dad, and I promptly forgot all about the experience.

At the time, my friends and I believed that an angel had probably placed the string exactly where we found it. We knew that God could and probably would help us, but we would not have lost our faith if He had not. Kids are like that. Theological questions are not complex.

Sometimes God says "Yes" and other times He says "No,"- end of discussion.

I lost track of my childhood friends long ago, but as for me, I've had an interesting journey. And through it all I still marvel that the King of the universe stooped to listen to three kids who had it right.

Chapter 32

Philosophical Musings

When I was small I enjoyed my mother's stories but sometimes I wondered. I remember my mother once looked at me with great surprise before exclaiming, "You are a skeptic!"

I had not experienced the wild things she read about and neither did I know anyone who had. I wanted to see for myself and wanted proof. And I decided that things written were no more plausible than things that were verbally related. In fact, words that are written in books can be the most deceptive of all.

However, I believed the Bible stories because they were in the Bible. My faith ebbed when I got older but strengthened again, and I will explain that process through some future stories. I know some readers will be able to relate; others will probably question my sanity.

My mother used to say that writers had a certain license—writer's privilege she called it. But I tend to think that the privilege should extend only to novels. I see no need to exaggerate or expand the facts when it is the intent to tell a true story.

When I was a teen-ager I was attracted to novels and mysteries but decided to stop reading them. There are so many amazing, true and informational books to read, that I decided I did not have time for the others. And there is a type of reading that makes it harder to concentrate on more serious fare.

This "True Tales" column is meant to include a variety of stories and some of them have already been of a religious or philosophical nature. If I did not include them I would be telling only a part of my experience. And for me, those stories are the most important of them all.

I am like the man in the Bible who came to Jesus and said, "If you can do anything, please help me." Jesus immediately picked up on that first little word and then the man said, "Please help my unbelief" (Luke 9:14-27). And that man wound up with a story to tell about how his request was granted.

We do not have to close our eyes or cover our ears in order to develop faith. I've told my children that they must find truth for themselves and faith should not be "blind." God invites people to ask questions.

My daughter took "organic chemistry" at Oregon State University and in the process, was asked how on earth she studied "evolution" at the smaller Christian college she also attended. She responded that the subject was treated as a theory. That the "theory" of evolution could be treated as such was a new thought to some of her fellow students.

In like manner, I do not expect readers to necessarily agree with my ideas or even to have knowledge of my particular philosophical or religious beliefs. But interspersed with a variety of stories and experiences will be some that have very definitely had a major impact on my life and way of thinking.

"Truth is stranger than fiction," my mother used to say, and I've found that to be quite true. She also said sometimes, "There are a lot of funny people out there, except for you and me." After a pause, and with a smirk, she would add, "And sometimes I wonder about you."

I've had my next story written for quite awhile. I'm going to share it, somewhat apprehensively, but it will pave the way for some others that I am also going to tell—I think. I'll decide later.

Chapter 33

The Key

After reading my story about the "green string," a visitor to Port Hardy had a comment for me. "I think you engaged in a little fantasy," he said. I told him that if he had found that story hard to believe, there was worse to come.

It seems like only a short time ago that I was about to enter the ninth grade after my parents had decided to send me to a private boarding school. We lived in a logging camp and I had completed the previous year by correspondence. So off I went to experience a new phase of growing up.

Except for the Christmas break, I did not see my family again until the school year was finished. I grew up fast and learned to cope with being homesick.

It was a church-operated school and most, but not all, of the students were from similar backgrounds. The older boy who shared my dorm room, went home one weekend, as did many of the other students and I was left to enjoy some peace and quiet.

On that particular Friday evening, my last activity before bed was a trip to the bathroom, just down the hall. As I opened my door, two students entered another room and I heard one of them say excitedly, "Put the key in Revelation!" The phrase meant nothing to me and I had no clue as to its meaning. I do not know why I remembered those words but they were the last words I heard that night.

Sometime later, I was awakened from a sound sleep and I was being suffocated. It was as if I was in a pressure chamber and the breath was being squeezed from my body. The very atmosphere was evil, and strangely, I knew immediately what was wrong. It was as if an urgent thought had been planted, and it consisted of one word, "pray."

Some people are quite concerned with the manner of prayer, words to use, who is to be addressed, and how to end. I had no time for that.

In my mind I simply screamed out to Jesus for help and I have never before or since received such instant relief.

Although no sound broke the awful gloom, it was like a silent gunshot shattered the atmosphere. With the speed of lightning, the evil presence vanished and there was perfect calm and peace. I did not even need to flip the light switch on.

I do remember kneeling in my bed as the tears flowed. I thanked the Lord from the depths of my heart before drifting off to a fearless and most wonderful sleep. And in time, the whole episode nearly vanished from my memory. My crisis of faith was still to come.

The boy who repeated the mystery phrase didn't seem to like me; I think it was a competition thing. There is a verse in the Bible that speaks of Jesus as holding the keys of hell and death. Although I did not know it at the time, ironically, this verse is sometimes used to invoke the name of Satan against another person.

Several years ago I learned of this fellow's whereabouts. I wrote to him and told him what I just told you. I told him that kids can do some of the craziest things and that I held no animosity. I told him how my faith had ebbed and flowed and I asked if he would be willing to verify or deny my story for the good of others. But to the time of this writing he has not replied.

Chapter 34

Witching Rods That Talk

The *North Island Gazette* of February 13, 1991, carried the story of Matt Graham, who was considered to be the top dowser in British Columbia. According to this article, he could find water and predict its depth and volume with his forked, copper, divining rod. Although many believe this ancient craft uses electrical and magnetic energy,

Matt believed the process to operate by way of mind power, as a God-given gift.

He typically began a search by holding a swinging plumb bob over a map. Later, in the field, he would ask his divining rod (wand) questions. "Yes" was indicated by an upward jerk. To quote from the article, "One of Graham's most well-known discoveries in the North Island is the spring that serves the needs of Port McNeill. He found it easily, after a drilling outfit had already spent several thousand dollars and many days drilling wells, coming up empty-handed each time."

When I was still in school, I wrote a short research paper on the subject of dowsing. I was curious but skeptical. To my surprise, I found an abundance of information in a wide variety of literature, including "scientific" journals and books.

I found that the craft can be traced back at least to ancient Egypt and has been used to find water, minerals, oil and even people. Some dowsers use a forked willow stick. Others use metal rods, broom handles or just their bare hands. And the really good dowsers only need a map. I found also, that Martin Luther condemned the practice of water witching or divining, as it is sometimes called.

I learned that while some people seem to have a natural and quick ability, anyone could become proficient with practice. Even Matt Graham was unsuccessful with his first try. *Organic Gardening* magazine told how Elmer Kulmar, although unable to perform the feat himself, was able to show his unbelieving wife how it was done. She easily found three wells for his orchard and even followed an underground stream to a more suitable well location. And this same article said that anyone could learn to dowse and that the dowsing rod would dip a number of times, indicating the depth to dig for water.

In the United States, hundreds of thousands of wells have been found using this method. In various parts of the world, people have become famous because of their finds in areas where there were no known reserves of water.

Native people had their mysterious power rods and twisted sticks too. The book, *Indian Healing*, tells how these paraphernalia were believed to have the ability to "twist things and men." A story is told of

84

one of these instruments twisting itself for the shaman doctor. And the doctors talked to these instruments just like Matt Graham talked to his.

Amazingly, Soviet scientists (apparently independently) developed a dowsing rod that looks very much like the Coast Salish Indian version. Is this science, coincidence or something else? The fact that the depth for water or minerals etc. could be known, bothered me. What if one was thinking in metric? Martin Luther's observations bothered me. And the Egyptian connection disturbed me too. I decided to buy some very expensive, precision, engineered dowsing rods.

Dowsing, witching, and divining are synonymous terms, but the "witching" and "divining" terminologies made me wonder. I had done enough research to know that witching for water actually could produce amazing results. So I waited impatiently for my expensive dowsing rods to arrive.

The Egyptian connection caused me to re-examine the Bible's Exodus story. In that account the Egyptian sorcerers were able to use some mystic power to make their rods turn into serpents, thus seeming to duplicate the miracle that God had performed (He had changed Moses' rod into a living serpent). But God's serpent ate the other serpents up.

As the story continues, Egypt was forced to its knees as the true God demonstrated that all other gods were false and deceptive. Because the serpent is a primary symbol for demonic involvement, God exposed the heart of Egypt's power.

Ancient gods are often shown with a serpent wrapped around their rods. The staff, or rod, of Aesculapius is always shown with a serpent entwined. This has become our modern medical symbol. It is fascinating to realize that old worship systems have a way of resurrecting themselves, in tangible ways, even in modern societies.

The ancient biblical admonition that God gave to His people after their deliverance from Egypt is largely ignored as outdated and irrelevant by our modern society. He said that it was an abomination to practice passing through the fire, divination, astrology, spells, witchcraft, wizardry, communication with familiar spirits or ghosts, or communication with anyone who has died (Deut. 18:10-12).

85

Today we call some of these things names like Ouija, crystal ball reading, tarot card reading, palm reading, teacup reading, psychic ability, channeling, automatic writing, yoga etc. When I bought my dowsing rods I did not know all of this. And I did not know that some people actually talked to their rods; but as a precaution, I told the Lord that if I was doing something wrong, to please protect me and to make the instruments fail. And they didn't perform at all. I returned them and had my money refunded.

It is intelligent information that is conveyed and I believe that this means of making contact with the unseen is just as forbidden now, as it was formerly. And the information is not acquired by electrical or magnetic energy, nor was that ever the case.

The Indians recognize a *spiritual* connection. Their stories of these instruments twisting themselves into a circular shape that crosses, reminds me of a serpent. And a successful Soviet version is so similar as to be uncanny.

A book called *The Art of Dowsing* explains that when one talks to the divining rod, "nature" responds. It also tells of a dowsing rod that twisted around itself three times. I find that interesting, especially in light of the fact that anciently the mystic number that the Bible warns against, was written as 666, SSS or shown as a serpent, pictured three times.

I was not convinced when I originally purchased my divination rods but I will have nothing to do with them now. I have come to believe that the biblical stories and admonitions, strange as they may be, should be taken just as they are written. God views the divination rod as a form of prostitution with a false god (Hosea 4:12).

I once explained my convictions to a pastor friend. In horror, he instinctively put his hand to his mouth and said, "The forked stick works for me." It does not make one evil to be deceived, but I fear that someone has a dangerous agenda and that this deception is a stepping-stone within a process that is very precise and purposeful. The word *occult* means *hidden* and there are hidden things that need to be exposed.

The book that reveals explains, "The great dragon was hurled down—that ancient serpent called the devil or Satan, who leads the whole world astray. He was hurled to the earth, and his angels with him" (Rev. 12:7, 9). Now, **that thought** leaves one with a lot to chew on.

Chapter 35

Sasquatch

It was August 19, 1995. We had sailed south along the inside passage from Prince Rupert and after passing numerous lakes and waterfalls, we pulled into Lowe Inlet. Grenville channel has several inlets branching off that lead into a land somehow frozen in time.

It is a lonely land that can be deathly, even frightfully, quiet and yet one is never really alone. At night the wolves howl though they are seldom seen in the daylight hours. The lonely cry of a raven is often the first sign of morning. If there should be the mewing of gulls, one welcomes the sound just because it breaks the awful silence.

At times a wind sweeps down from the mountains, whistling through the treetops, but the sound is neither soothing nor reassuring. In fact, it seems to speak of secrets that can never be unlocked. Oh yes, occasionally there is the sudden honking of geese disturbed, or the splash of seals as they seek to startle—on purpose. Usually their heads simply *appear* on the surface of the water and then suddenly vanish with scarcely a ripple to mark the spot. Sometimes tiny murreletts can be heard peeping as they take time out from fishing.

We dropped anchor at the head of Lowe Inlet where Kumowdah River becomes Verney Falls. At low tide, the water rushes down and over the rocks filling this otherwise hushed land with a kind of violent noise and action. "Kumowdah" is an Indian name and the chart uses other Native names such as Kumealon, Kxngeal and Klewnugget.

There is evidence of ancient human activity. Numerous rocks and boulders have been stacked to form a circular wall, leaving the shoreline near the river, and returning to another point on the same shore. The rocks are covered at high tide but at low tide they once formed a trap. I noticed salmon jumping in exactly the spot where people of long ago must have observed the same. Fortunately for the salmon of today, the rock wall is broken and not complete. So if they escape modern nets and hooks at sea, they have only to face treacherous falls, hungry seals, otters, bears—and eagles.

Eagles love nice juicy salmon. I once stole a big Coho from an eagle and left him the head. From the screeching I heard, I was led to believe that he had desired more. But I'm sure he knew that life in the wilds can be rough. Only the biggest and best survive. Eagles have often drowned trying to flop a big fish to shore. In my case, the eagle had fought his fish to shore, but had not yet been able to enjoy the fruits of his labors. I did that for him after smiling and thanking him profusely. I'm glad I did not understand his response. But I had the feeling that the whole silent country heard about my less admirable qualities.

Salmon were trying to scale the falls and as the tide rose, more and more attempted the seemingly hopeless task. Some were flipped sideways and others were tossed head over tail by the rushing water. Several even landed on the rocks. I sat and watched as seals caught and ate fish after fish. I was amazed with how little time it took to consume a large salmon. As the seals jumped and played with their prey, the rushing water muffled the sounds of their activity. Obviously bears had fished the rapids and obviously they had been eating many berries as well as salmon. Their excrement (bear sign) told the story. Otters also caught fish beneath the falls. The fish were vulnerable until the tidal water rose high enough that they could jump the higher rapids.

I decided to enter the country to which the fish were journeying, so I traversed the falls and followed the shoreline of a lake. The sound of roaring water became fainter and fainter and a sense of solitude began to engulf me. I lost track of time and became absorbed with the rugged scenery. A high rock mountain could be seen on one side and the lake seemed to take a turn. I desired to hike until I could see how far up the valley the lake extended. I climbed above the lake and when by chance I looked down and forward of my line of travel, I was startled and instantly, focused.

To my surprise, I was not the only person in this God-forsaken land. A stooped man walked with his back to me. I could hear no sound of his walking in spite of the fact that the eerie silence was so complete. I assumed that he was too far away but wondered why *no* sound could be heard. Surely a twig should snap or bushes rustle. And there was something else about him.

Although he walked upright, something was peculiar... there was something about his clothing - no color, or same color - a drab brown - everything brown, head to toe. And then it hit me; that was it - head to toe, **brown** - head to toe, including head, including toes, or at least feet, because I couldn't really see his toes. The clothing had to be of one piece and perhaps some type of fur.

The man stopped (I just *assumed* a man - certainly *not* a woman, out there, alone) and appeared to be in thought. Instinctively, I crouched low as he slowly turned. I knew he could not have seen me. I was the observer and he the observed but he raised his head and looked in my direction. Two things struck me with horror.

His face resembled a man's and yet it was not a man's face. I do not know how to describe it, except to say that it was somewhat human and somewhat (for lack of a better word) ape-like, but that does not adequately describe it. Perhaps I should just say that there was a wild animal-like look to his features. His face was hairy and could almost have been a man's if it was shaved.

The second thing that startled me and increased my heart's rapid beating was when he slowly raised his hand and waved something at me. It appeared to be a stick or perhaps a small club, as it was rounded and bulged at one end. I was amazed that he seemed to know that I had been watching him. For a moment I thought perhaps he was looking and waving menacingly at something else, but he kept staring in my direction—and I had thought that I was all alone. I quietly and slowly glanced around to see if there was something or somebody that would take the heat off me. I was very unnerved; it seemed as if this barren land perhaps was not so barren as it seemed; it was alive with who-knows-what. Where was I and what was was I doing here?

As I returned my now thoroughly frightened gaze to meet his steady and expressionless stare, he turned and disappeared behind a large cedar tree. I don't know how long I waited for him to reappear, but when he did not, I decided to carefully walk to where I could view the other side of the tree. As I did not want to get close, I had to maintain my distance and advantage on the hill while keeping my eyes fixed on the tree. I walked until I could see the far side of the tree. There was nothing there, absolutely nothing. Where was the man, the thing, it?

I wanted only to be out of there. This place was not barren, silent, and lonely. It was alive. Things were everywhere. I could not see them but I could feel them. I thought I heard things, I thought I saw things - subtle things - little movements, like salal bushes moving when something has just been there. I am still not sure of what was real and what was imagined - except for the strange man. I did not imagine him.

There is something about that country. On the one hand, it holds an almost irresistible attraction, and on the other hand, it holds a sense of foreboding. The wind was right—there *are* secrets in that strange, quiet land. Perhaps someday I will return; I want to return, at least I think I do, but not right away.

I first related this tale to my wife Linda, and her friend Karen, when I returned from my hike and while we sat beneath the same Verney Falls. Linda pried the details from me when she perceived that something was bothering me. I reluctantly and haltingly told the story in bits and pieces—after extracting a promise from both of them—that our conversation would remain confidential. Then I fell silent and looked out to sea.

My wife watched me intently; in fact she stared at me and studied my expression. I could see her out of the corner of my eye and I tried not to meet her gaze. I must have slipped just the tiniest expression of a smile - because she suddenly snorted in disgust, and shook her head. While Karen looked confused, I doubled over with laughter and rolled on the rocks.

Chapter 36

The Last Laugh

All my stories are as true and accurate as I know how to make them and that includes the previous tale. But I'm sure you realize that the real story is in the last paragraph. Yes, my wife believed the whole yarn and that *is* the story. Perhaps you, the reader, got caught up in the telling, like she did. There was no Sasquatch but if you were to go to Lowe Inlet you would see that my description is accurate and there almost *could* be a Bigfoot nearby.

I did not believe in Sasquatch stories when I spun my yarn, and paid no attention to them, but the last laugh may have been on me. Let me explain by telling you about my friend, Mark. He is an American who lived briefly on the North Island. I met him at a campfire on Stories Beach and his first question for me was whether or not I knew anyone who had seen a Sasquatch.

Mark had been captivated as a teenager and knew all the books and authors on the subject. He had popped in to see biologist, Dr. John Bindernagel, of Courtenay, who had just written the most recent book - North America's Great Ape: The Sasquatch. Dr. Bindernagel had given him the names of some contacts in Port Hardy and Mark wondered if I could help track them down.

As for me, after the initial chuckle, I remembered an employee who had fished with me about ten years previous. He had told me a story that seemed incredible and I had not really paid much attention. But he had been very disturbed at the time and seemed embarrassed and yet needed to talk.

I found a phone number and made the call. Gordon said that he had regretted ever telling me the story and had wondered for ten years what I thought of him. He assured me that he had not imbibed any spirits or inhaled any smoke of any kind at the time of his encounter and he just wanted me to know that.

When I told him about other stories I was hearing and gave him Bindernagel's Web site, he agreed to write his experience and even said that I could use his name. I have found this to be true in all cases except for one man who just happens to be the subject of the very first story in Bindernagel's book. Most people are relieved to find that there are many other people who share similar experiences. Here is Gordon's story in his own words.

Hi, all, OK, I was checking out hunting territory at night by using a spotlight (ya ya, I know it was illegal) on the roadside as I traveled to my campsite for the night. The place was just a few clicks south of Sayward (heading to Hardy) on the right hand side of the Island Highway. It is past the little provincial park but just before Sayward.

I shone the spotlight into the woods on the left side of the logging road (about 3 clicks off the island highway) and saw an upright "animal" about 30 feet from my truck. This "animal" remained upright as I shone the light on it; it raised its arms to protect its eyes (or so I thought); then it did an amazing 4-6 foot side step behind a medium sized fir or cedar tree. It was like a basketball player dodging to the right to defend his zone; very nimble, very quick.

It does not sound like much. However, as a hunter of 20+ years at that time, it was a new and truly frightening experience. I have never seen anything like it before .. or after. It lasted maybe 3 to 5 seconds .... It scared the daylights out of me. It had what I would say was long hair (about 12 inches or so) hanging off its upper limbs from the elbow to the body. The top of its head was narrow, and it had longish hairs coming off its jaw area. I did not get a good look at any facial features. Perspective is important and I did not have that since it was dark, so I cannot truly guesstimate the size ... All I know is that it scared me so bad I stopped using that night checkout routine for areas I want to hunt later. (deckhand—Gordon)

Someone said that I should talk to Clarence, who I knew. He said that some years earlier he and his brother had been commercial fishing and anchored their boats in an isolated bay on the Central Coast—in Mussel Inlet. Just as daylight was breaking he heard what he thought was a woodpecker until he realized that he was hearing wood hitting wood. Then the same sound answered from another part of the forest and this repeated from different areas in the hills. He woke his brother to come and listen and in the dead quiet of the early morning it was rather eerie.

The Native village of Klemtu was not far away and he later asked residents for an explanation. Someone named George Brown reported that stick beating was a known characteristic of Sasquatch and that famous Native guide, Clayton Mack, had confirmed the practice. Local residents had seen the creatures and in the book *Grizzlies and White Guys*, Clayton had reported three encounters.

A Port Hardy man, who was featured in Bindernagel's book, was more than happy to tell me his story as long as I promised not to use his name in a written version. He said that he had seen a Sasquatch in the trees at the Eagle Nest rest stop down by Woss. They locked eyes for awhile and he got a good look at the creature and said that he would never forget the way it spun to face him.

The long hair on it's back fanned out as it turned. And then it ran on two legs through the trees like there was no forest to impede it. He said he has often asked himself if he was dreaming and has put up with lots of laughter and poking even from his own family. But he said that he has spent many years in the woods and has worked with wildlife officials and that he is observant and used to wildlife. And this experience occurred in broad daylight and his son saw the creature too.

Since Native people often have stories, I asked some friends if they had any. It turned out that their son claimed to have seen a Sasquatch cross the upper Island Highway at night. It had leaped out of the darkness and crossed the road with two quick strides. The family told jokes every time they passed the location until two other family members pulled over one night at the Eagle Nest rest stop. In the darkness, something was shaking the trees and the two family members jumped back in their car and peeled out.

My American friend was doing his own research and we were comparing notes at a church potluck. A woman overheard us talking and informed us that she had seen a Sasquatch. I was incredulous and asked, "Where?" "Between Woss and Sayward - on the Island Highway - at night - and the thing was across the road in about two quick steps." Kathy said that her husband had been laughing ever since. But I can tell you, that he, like me, is not laughing quite so loudly anymore.

Another opportunity presented itself when Pastor Johnston came to visit. He had grown up in Takush, a Native village where his mother taught school. Chief George took a liking to him and told him many stories, amongst which, were stories of the wild man of the forest. Pastor Johnston thought that he had used the name "umpsumps" but most coastal Natives use a word that sounds like Bukwus or Boqs. The chief told him that the creature would dig clams at night and after very low tides. It could move fast but would sometimes hunch up and the creature's long hair made it look very much like a seaweed-covered rock.

One morning, after an extreme low tide, the chief told him to come with him in a little boat. He didn't explain why but he followed the shore and appeared to be looking for something. Then he pulled into a little mud cove and told Frank to get out. "Do you see anything?" he asked. Frank did not, but after some prodding he noticed some tracks. After some more prodding he decided that they were bear tracks. The chief sat silent for some time before snorting, "Huh, pretty funny bear don't you think that walks on two legs?"

Frank took a closer look and was shocked to see large tracks similar to the tracks that people would leave and the tracks were made by a creature that walked on two legs. And one day his dog disappeared for several days. When it returned the hair on one side of its body was all torn off. It would not enter the forest after that.

Pastor Johnston wrote his next experience out for me and I am going to quote from a few parts of it. It was many years later and he was gillnetting in Smith Inlet:

"Though the moon was full, its heavenly position in relationship with McBride Bay dictated that the southern shore of the bay was shrouded in complete blackness once all daylight was gone. Because salmon fishermen alone on their boats can only eat whenever they get a chance; due to their demanding work, I chose to hang on the shoreward end of my net during slack low tide and make myself a good, belated supper.

The Last Laugh

As I shut off the engine and went below, Caesar became more and more restless. Deep in his throat he kept up a steady menacing, yet fearful, growling -- and this from a dog that wasn't afraid to tackle a young cougar at one point in his past. I tried to get him to join me in the cabin, but he refused.

Not long after I went below, suddenly, my canine companion who was known far and wide for his quietness broke into volleys of vicious barking. Calling to him made no impact upon him and after a short time I decided to investigate the source of his uneasiness. As I approached him on deck, I saw that, he stood with his front paws on the gun'l, the hair along his back stood up stiff and menacingly as he faced the shore not far away. Curious as to what might be there, I returned to the wheelhouse and picking up my hand held search light, I directed its powerful beam through the window closest to the point ashore that was attracting the excited dog.

Slowly I played the beam over the bare flats. Plainly visible were scattered gray-granite boulders covered with silvery barnacles and generously endowed with amber seaweed. Though the glass through which my light penetrated returned a disconcerting glow into my eyes, the view was still plain enough for me to see that that there didn't appear to be anything unusual -- or was there? Suddenly the beam of the light played on a bolder that seemed somewhat larger than the largest of the others and reflected not a glimmer of the silvery-gray, and the "seaweed" looked to be more like hair and a much darker colour.

With intense curiosity and determined to see "it" more plainly, I switched off the light and as quickly as possible I unfastened the coiled extension of the cord so that it would reach out onto the deck where I hastened. During these few moments Caesar's barking and movements became so intense that I half expected him to jump overboard, but the note of fear in his bark reassured me that he probably wouldn't. Then with the cord free and in the open air I again switched on my light and trained it onto the spot I had viewed from the wheelhouse window. The "rock" was gone!

Frantically, I played the beam up the beach toward the forest and back and forth along the flats. Nothing! Well, that's my story. What did I see? What excited my dog? In the dark of the night and with my dog so wildly worked up, I did not go ashore and search for tracks!"

It was a year or two after my hearing this story that Andy, a son of Chief George, lay dying in the hospital of throat cancer. He couldn't speak but I went to visit him and to try to encourage him as he faced imminent death. Somewhere along the way I shared the previous story and asked if his dad had shared the same information with him. To my surprise he just smiled and shook his head, no.

I returned the next day and he motioned for a pen and paper. On the paper he wrote, "You are looking at someone who saw one." I didn't understand and asked, "You?" He shook his head and pointed to his wife who was sitting nearby in the same chair she had occupied the day before.

Although I could now fill a small book with Sasquatch stories, most of them are volunteered by people who hear that others have shared their story first. I guess Kathy decided that I was safe; she proceeded to tell me that she saw one when she was a little girl over at Blunden Harbour, another village site—across from Port Hardy. It was smashing clams and shells before it stood up on a rock and looked at her grandfather and her. Then it ran into the woods.

Many of the old Native elders are not at all surprised at these stories. I have been told of food and clothing being taken, of Sasquatch peering in windows… And I am told that it is not unusual, at some of the old village sites, to have rocks thrown on the roofs.

My next story is so strange that I am going to include it in its own chapter just as it was written and sent to me. Here's the background. I was sharing with my elderly uncle who had spent his life in the woods and I could see that he was smiling politely. I understood that look but suddenly his son—my cousin—who I grew up with, told such a wild story that I immediately decided to check it out before he could compare notes with another friend who had shared the experience.

I found Roland's phone number (I hadn't talked to him for years) and filled him in on what I was learning. I included some interesting tidbits concerning Native beliefs, shared around the world, that link the Sasquatch to death and an element of the Supernatural. Then I asked if he had been present and could verify the story that Dennis had shared with me.

There was a long pause before he affirmed and said that just listening to me had sent chills up his spine. Incidentally, when I asked Dennis why he had never shared the story before, he replied by way of a question. "Would you have told anyone if it had happened to you?" he asked.

Chapter 37

The Horrible Scream

(Murray-Good talking to you the other night, I thought I would put my recollections down and send them to you. Thinking about that day so long ago still gives me the chills.)

First some background to the story. Maybe you were even in on this but several of us were hiking, or walking along the right side of Sea lion bay (as you enter) and there are several cliffs in that area. Below one of those cliffs we found a primitive campsite. Fire remains, a pile of branches for a bed, needles long since fallen off, and beside that bed an old wool coat laid lengthwise along the bed. This camp was tucked up under the cliff and was very dry and protected, actually dusty as I remember thinking that so unusual for the coast. It made quite an impression on me and I thought about it often, was it a stranded traveler? A logger whose boat simply quit and he needed a spot to sleep while waiting for rescue? Someone marooned waiting in vain for rescue? In my young and fertile mind this seemed to fit the best. Why else would he leave his nice heavy wool coat behind, something you need on the coast even in summer? I was drawn back to the spot sometime later to look around some more, I thought I may find something, A jackknife, lighter, bones, whatever. It was kind of spooky by myself but I poked at the coat and was surprised that my fingers went right through it, it was so decayed that it turned to dust at

97

the slightest touch, an indicator that it had been there a long time and that the area was very well protected from the elements, as a good rain would have washed it all away. I took a button from it, had it for years but have no idea where it is now. I wish now that I would have thought to check the pockets. Anyway that was a very long and tedious story to get to the part you are interested in.

I mentioned the coat story to Dennis and he expressed a desire to see it. This may have been the year us kids were doing the Logging, with Ernie there to make sure we didn't kill each other. I don't remember what year that was, but it was a year or two before I went fishing with Gary.

After work one day we took one of the work boats, the old 40 horse Johnson running smoothly through the glass smooth water as we rounded the corner into the bay. Just about the time I was ready to throttle down and turn toward shore the engine quit. Just as if someone had pushed the off switch, except I don't remember those old engines having such a luxury. Seems to me we had to choke it to get it stopped. As we coasted to a stop the echoes from the noisy outboard faded away and it was deathly quiet. We were probably both lost in thought about "now what? Gas? Plugs? Do we have a paddle?" Neither of us had said a word to break the silence when the most bone chilling sound came from the direction of the cliffs that had been our destination, a human sounding scream/maniacal laugh echoed out over the bay, mouths agape we began to look at each other when movement caught our attention. At the head of the bay you remember Don Kaufman had logged a little A-frame claim. Through the corner of the claim walked a creature. It walked into the water, swam across a small corner of the bay, walked out of the water and disappeared into the woods. Here is what I remember about that short encounter. It was pale or dirty white in color. The color seemed to come from hair. It walked upright on hind legs. As it walked out of the water, water streamed off of it. I could not tell how long the hair was. I did not discern any specific facial features. It was not a bear. I don't remember any sound, not even water cascading off or branches breaking underfoot. At best guess it was about 200 yards away, too far to guess height but the impression was taller than a normal human. It never looked at us but it is ludicrous to think it didn't know we were there.

After a time Dennis and I looked at each other, he with a thunderstruck expression on his face, my mouth was dry and I remember trying to swallow, we had the expected conversation, did you see that, are we seeing things, etc. I find it interesting that neither of us has told anyone about this encounter. I still feel like people will think I'm nuts. I mean really, Sea Lion Bay? What a macabre set of circumstances. I have told the story around the campfire up to the horrible scream several times, and that seemed plenty strange to most. To top it off the stalled outboard motor started smoothly on the first pull of the starter rope. Our exploration plans were derailed and we went back to camp.

What was it? Why did it enter the water for such a short swim? Why didn't it look at us? Was the scream connected to the creature? Was the motor stopping just a huge coincidence? It would be interesting to have Dennis read this and see if he remembers it similarly, it sounds as if at least the basics of our recollections match.

Anyway that's about it unless you have some specific questions.

Take care, Roland

It was several years again and Roland and his dad were staying at my home for the weekend. We were sharing some old stories and I told a few Squatch tales. Roland was very quiet and it seemed as if the whole subject was new to his dad; in fact he said that if he ever saw such a thing he would immediately think it was demonic. So I was careful and did not share too much. Later I sent an email to Roland and asked about my hunch. Here is a part of his reply:

"You are right about the story, I haven't told my dad, I actually haven't told anybody although I did let Gayle read a copy of the letter I sent to you. It is very difficult for me to talk about it; it seemed easier to write it down. Even after all these years I get chills and my heart starts racing when I think about it or start to talk about it. Having said that it is probably time I got over it. Maybe it wouldn't be so bothersome out in the open. I think some folks wonder about your sanity when they hear something like that"...

Roland, I thought you might be interested to know that I went back to Sealion Bay and for the first time that I remember, there were no seals. It was a typical dripping wet coastal day and it was very, very quiet as usual. Kevin and I hiked through the wet woods to the cliff and cave. It was still pretty awesome but after all these years I could find no sign of boots, clothing or campfire. Thanks for sharing your story, Murray.

I am going to come back to this subject but first I am going to share some other Native stories that may be different but similar, and they may connect. We will see.

Chapter 38

The Roamer

For years, a pretty seine boat called the "Roamer" was featured on a postcard. I began my career as a fishing master on this vessel. Unfortunately my career was marred by a sinking when this little ship settled to the bottom, 130 feet beneath the waves.

My first fishing season was a financial disaster and the only thing that could have made it worse was to sink. That happened the second year, at the beginning of the season, when we slammed full force into the rocks. And I had been enjoying such a good sleep too.

I would hasten to point out that I was fast asleep in my bunk; it was my crewman who was sleeping at the wheel. And I was shocked to find him still slumped over the steering wheel when I rushed forward, screaming like a madman. Joe was dazed and speechless when our searchlight revealed only rocks and branches of trees all around us.

I yanked the throttle back, as the boat was still pushing full speed ahead but going nowhere.

I managed to back the boat off the rocks but was horrified to find water gushing into the engine room and I couldn't tell from where. The pumps did not stand a chance. I told my wife and Joe to get the skiff ready while I sought to notify the authorities of our plight. I was unable to raise the Coast Guard but did make contact with a gill-netter in River's Inlet. I told him it looked as though we were somewhere across from Namu. Then I prepared to abandon ship.

I was running through a mental list of things to do when I suddenly realized that we were missing two of our crew. In disbelief, and with my heart in my throat, I descended a ladder into the flooding engine room and opened a door that led to the forward sleeping quarters. The engine was still running, so I flicked on a light and yelled. The two sixteen year olds were fast asleep in their bunks! To this day, I marvel at the strangeness of it all. Jerry was a black lad. He thought I was joking until his feet got wet. I will never forget his big white eyeballs in the dim light. Then, we waded through the icy water.

The rest is a bit of a blur but I remember the engine stopping and the hiss of steam and the lights going out and the gurgle as the old ship disappeared from sight. And I remember the awful quiet and the sick feeling in the pit of my stomach and the full moon.

Way off in the distance we could see the lights of some American boats heading for Alaska. We shot off an emergency rocket that lit up the whole sky, but the boats just kept going. Finally one turned and rescued us. The men thought we had been celebrating. "Celebrating?" we asked. "Yeah", they replied. "It's the 4th of July."

Most of us were able to get immediate jobs on other boats. Joe got a job on a packer but it sank on his very first trip the next week. Another time he had two opportunities to go for a fall opening out at Nit Nat on the West Coast of Vancouver Island. But he missed the first boat and caught the second—*Karena #1*. Its anchor line snapped while the crew was sleeping and it smashed on the beach with no loss of life. When he checked on the other boat, *Kingfisher I*, he learned that it had sunk the same day.

Then there was the time Joe stepped on a nail just before he was to go halibut fishing. He was actually steering the boat *Pacific Traveler* out to the grounds while the skipper slept, but was forced to turn around because of the infection in his foot. Good thing, because when that boat went out again, it capsized in a terrible southeasterly storm.

When the *Pacific Traveler* rolled over, the skipper, Leonard Egolf lost his life. Joe's replacement, Randy Morrison, was rescued, but just barely.

Joe's little gillnet vessel swamped once while being towed. But other than that, his most recent sinking was in the fall of 1998 (as far as I know) on a boat called the *Pula*. I call him Jonah but Joe is fairly confidant that the worst is behind him. We'll see.

I have one more boat story, and this one concerns a "mystical" or "spirit" boat. Shortly before Randy Morrison was rescued by helicopter, a small boat, something like a canoe came by. There were some old men in it and they told Randy it was time for him to join them. At first I thought that Randy liked publicity and knew how to tell a good story, but then I learned some things that make his story much more interesting. Have you ever had a near- death experience? Or has someone from the dead, or "spirit" world made contact with you?

Most of the world is not surprised at these things. And according to Gallup polls about three quarters of Americans believe in some aspect of the paranormal.

Chapter 39

Spirit Ship

It is those awful "sou-easters" that have so often caused havoc with mariners. It was a horrible Southeast storm that brought about the demise of the sturdy little salmon and halibut boat, "Pacific Traveller."

This fishing trip seemed fraught with bad omens from the beginning. With only two people aboard, the boat had been forced to return to port when the crewman's foot became infected. The boat had to return again when his replacement became incapacitated due to seasickness. This is how Randy Morrison found himself aboard. The pressure was on, because the fishing time was limited and there were only several openings in any given year.

You can read this gripping tale in the book *Dangerous Waters*. I knew the skipper who lost his life in this accident, but there is another aspect to this story that caught my attention. Although the skipper drowned, Randy Morrison survived hours of agony because he had an immersion suit.

Shortly before his rescue, he had a fascinating spiritual experience or hallucination or *something*. He was interviewed on radio and featured in various magazines. At first I smiled, and thought he was a very good storyteller.

According to Randy, a rowboat or canoe-like vessel approached him with some old men in it. They told him to get in, but sort of telepathically, because they did not speak. He put his hand out, but his hand went through the boat, which is when he realized it was a *spirit* boat. He knew instinctively that he was about to join these men in death—on the other side. And then the helicopter arrived; it was close.

Later, I was amazed to find a widespread teaching around the world that makes his story much more interesting. Virtually all the ancient cultures and religions had a *River of Life* and when you crossed this river, you entered death—a mystical new realm of *spirit*. Life simply took a new form; mind and thought—the essence of who you are, did not cease. Death was (is) not an enemy or anything to be feared. In fact, it could be a joyous new passage.

The symbol associated with this crossing was a *boat*. You may have read of various archaeological discoveries where boats have been found buried with the dead. This has been the case in China, Scandinavia, Egypt and England. *And the Coast Salish people used to bury their dead in a canoe.*

Another symbol related to life- after- death teachings, was *Sun* representing the ultimate God or power source. Various inter-related and even synonymous deities of the nations had their source in the Sun. And the Sun is daily and yearly reborn. *Easter* and *Christmas* traditions have their origins here, long before Christianity adapted them to new purpose.

The *serpent* represents wisdom, protection, enlightenment, power, and is closely associated with Sun worship and life- after- death beliefs. The serpent was often represented as having wings, and jewellery was patterned after the likeness of serpent and sun. In art, the serpent is often shown encircling the sun. (A circle never ends) The dragon is simply a volatile form of the serpent.

The *cross* is also associated with serpent and sun. The cross has always represented the link between heaven and earth and life-after-death ideas. Thus, the cross is often depicted within a solar disk. The Egyptian ankh and Hitler's swastika are variations of the cross, which comes from Tammuz, the reincarnated and ancient Nimrod sun god. Another form of the cross is found in the three-pronged trident, source of the idea for the devil's pitchfork.

The Egyptian root word for the Sun was "Ra." This was found in the ruler's name. And it is found in the word cobra. The dead Pharaoh had a winged snake undulating the whole length of his coffin, representing the immortality of the soul.

Throughout history a class of mystic healers, known as shamans, or medicine men, trained in the healing arts. They also possessed knowledge of the supernatural and could contact spirits. Our medical symbol finds its' origin here. You've seen the intertwining serpents. And don't they have wings? Variations of the name for Shaman are found throughout the world. Interestingly, the name for the Sun god of the Assyro-Babylonian religion was *Shamash*. This god was worshiped as the author of justice and compassion.

Actually, although the caduceus, with its' wings and twin snakes is a recognized medical symbol, it is really the staff of Asklepios, (Greek) Aesculapius, (Roman) with a single snake entwined, that is the true symbol of medicine. Aesculapius was the son of the sun god Apollo. Aesculapius was the god of healing and was believed to have the power not only to prevent death, but also to raise the dead to life. He was able to metamorphose into a snake, thus the origin of the staff of Aesculapius.

The Norsemen conducted trade and commerce with a symbolic winged serpent ship. But war was waged with dragon boats. Closer to home, the Indians did not go into or out of their long- houses without passing under Sisutl, the double-headed serpent or double-headed dragon. At least *some* coastal tribes had a ceremony where the Shamans *paddled* to the land of the dead in order to make contact. This would be to the west.

The Egyptian's River of Life was the Nile. The east side was for the living but the west side, the burial side, was known as the land for the dead.

So what, you say? Hang on. The plot thickens.

Chapter 40

The Reality of Myth

Joseph Campbell may be the world's foremost mythologist. For this article, I've adapted one of his book titles from "The *Power* of Myth" to "The *Reality* of Myth."

Campbell says, "Freud, Jung and their followers have demonstrated irrefutably that the logic, the heroes, and the deeds of myth survive into modern times. In the absence of an effective general mythology, each of us has his private unrecognized, rudimentary, yet secretly potent pantheon of dream" (*The Hero With a Thousand Faces*, p. 4).

Joseph Campbell came to the shocking conclusion that the shared stories and experiences, told round the world, spring forth *independently* and *spontaneously*... "out of the common ground of what C.G. Jung has termed the collective unconscious" (*The Inner Reaches of Outer Space,* p. 91). This is how he explained the serpent ideas, and especially the double-headed serpent symbolism with associated beliefs.

These various researchers seem to be suggesting that the world's stories, fairy tales and myths, including those from the biblical Judeo-Christian tradition, come from the shared experience of human evolutionary development. This "mystery" is somehow stored in our *subconscious* or *unconscious*.

The dictionary definition of myth has to do with a story or stories, told round the world, with a common theme that has some message for us. A different usage for the word is when it is used to describe something that is untrue or unbelievable.

There are books and even encyclopedias dealing with the world's mythologies, but most do not explain the strange and sometimes bizarre realities that spring from the various beliefs and teachings.

The word "myth" if used all-inclusively, may be somewhat of a misnomer.

Consider these excerpts taken from the "Travel" section of the Vancouver Sun newspaper: "The Vegetarian festival on Thailand's resort island of Phuket isn't for the squeamish. Amid showers of firecrackers, men and some women march through town with long skewers piercing their cheeks, earlobes and arms.

"Then, with heads shaking and eyes rolling, they walk ankle-deep in burning coals or bathe in hot cooking oil. Some laugh hysterically as they sit on chairs of nails; others, in a trance, climb ladders fitted with knife blade rungs.

"They shake their heads and froth at the mouth as, according to local beliefs, a god possesses them and allows them to endure wounds and heat without pain.

"Once in the trance, the devotees chatter in high squeaky Chinese even though they themselves are Thais and no longer speak their ancestors' language.

"The men marching with skewers in their skin wore aprons with fearsome dragons and the Chinese names of their favorite gods embroidered on red, green or yellow silk.

"Some bounded across—the fastest left only three hot footprints in the bed of coals—while others walked slowly or even danced around, kicking up flames with each step" (Tom Heneghan, *The Vancouver Sun,* Nov. 1, 1986).

Closer to home, I remember a couple of years ago, my boat had been dry docked and I was returning by ferry from Sointula to Port McNeil. I was dozing after a hard day and awoke to an animated conversation. A woman was telling a group of listeners how she had been to see a person who knew everything about her, even secret things. It was uncanny. The speaker described in amazement and bewilderment how predictions had been made which seemed to be accurate. And then she added that this other woman's house was filled with figurines of serpents and dragons.

Have you noticed how often these creatures are depicted in comics, cartoons, toys, movies, games and books? They are often linked to fantasy or horror. And fantasy games like "Dungeons and Dragons" are known to have an addictive element and can produce noticeable personality changes.

I did not become involved in the conversation just described. I wish I had but felt that my input might not have been appreciated.

I remember the sense of wonder and awe I felt when as a boy, I explored some of our coastal inlets. The loggers sometimes stumbled upon ancient burial grounds. I've seen the cedar-bark rope and blankets and long weasel-skin robes of the Shaman medicine men. And I've seen Sisustl the serpent, fashioned into a form where the mouth holds the tail just like the Egyptians depict. It is the universal story of the circle of life, and a circle never ends.

In Babylon the serpent was known as Aesculapius—the life restorer. The Aztecs called him Quetzalcoatl, meaning *feathered serpent*. Quetzalcoatl was the personification of the planet Venus as both the *Morning Star* and the Evening Star. His Mayan name was Kukulcan. "Kulkul" means "beautiful bird," and "Can," serpent.

Coastal natives called him Siskiu or Sisutl. He's known as the double-headed serpent or double-headed dragon and is sometimes depicted with a crescent, representative of wings in other cultures. The stories tell of his ability to fly and change form, to human. He is beneficial, but can become malevolent if angered.

Anciently, magicians were priests who claimed to possess occult (hidden) knowledge. "Diviner" is translated from the Greek puthon from which we get the word "python." A python guarded the Delphic oracle, which was used to predict the future. A pythoness was a priestess of Apollo.

I used to ask Robert Walkus (now deceased) about some of the old beliefs and once I asked him if Sisutl was actually seen. After a long pause, he told me the old people used to see him in Long Lake where the Smith Inlet Indians harvested sockeye. Then he told me other stories, which he seemed to accept as having actually happened. Many of our Native friends, both past and present, have a strong belief in the world of spirits.

Out-of-body experiences, near-death experiences and meditation experiences, all seem to share the same mystical supercharged energy force. Eastern religion calls this force "kundalini" represented as a serpent that rises up the spine to activate the brain.

Out of body experience is termed "astral" travel or astral projection. The experience is often described as a sensation of leaving one's body and even viewing it in a detached manner. The person may see things in distant places and eavesdrop on private conversations that are later verified.

Numerous books and articles tell with excitement, how these stories seem to be exploding across our society. The National Film Board of Canada has videos on the subject. And in the past, our own "North Island News" has had a continued feature on the Metaphysics, where we have been given information on what supposedly takes place at death, and how to contact the dead through spirit guides, channeling etc. Without doubt, some of you who read this, will have had experience in some of these areas, or will know someone who has.

Remember the concepts of light, sun, illumination, wisdom, tree of life, river of life, serpent, dragon…

Chapter 41

Joseph Campbell

The late Joseph Campbell has affected our thinking perhaps more than we realize. He was an author and lecturer, and probably the most recognized authority in the field of mythology. As well, he was the inspiration behind the "Star Wars" movies, in which George Lucas sought (with the Force) to convey what Carl Jung referred to as the "archetype of the collective unconscious." Following are quotations taken from an interview with Lucas as reported in *Time* magazine, April 26, 1999.

"Moyers: Joseph Campbell once said all the great myths, the ancient great stories, have to be regenerated in every generation. He said that's what you are doing with Star Wars. You are taking these old stories and putting them into the most modern of idioms, the cinema. Are you conscious of doing that? Or are you first setting out to make a good action-movie adventure?

Lucas: With Star Wars, I consciously set about to re-create myths and the classic mythological motifs. I wanted to use those motifs to deal with issues that exist today. The more research I did, the more I realized that the issues are the same ones that existed 3000 years ago. That we haven't come very far emotionally.

Moyers: Is one religion as good as another?

Lucas: I would say so. Religion is basically a container for faith. And faith in our culture, our world and on a larger issue, the mystical level-which is God, what one might describe as a supernatural, or the things that we can't explain- is a very important part of what allows us to remain stable, remain balanced.

Lucas: I put the Force into the movie in order to try to awaken a certain kind of spirituality in young people-more a belief in God than a belief in any particular religious system. I wanted to make it so that young people would begin to ask questions about the mystery…

Lucas: …I wanted to try to explain in a different way the religions that have already existed. I wanted to express it all.

Moyers: You're creating a new myth?

Lucas: I'm telling an old myth in a new way. Each society takes that myth and retells it in a different way…

Lucas: Ultimately the Force is the larger mystery of the universe. And to trust your feelings is your way into that."

Joseph Campbell has written, "Reviewing with unprejudiced eye the religious traditions of mankind, one becomes very soon aware of certain mythic motifs that are common to all, though differently understood and developed in the differing traditions: ideas, for example, of a life beyond death, or of malevolent and protective spirits" (*The Inner Reaches of Outer Space*, p. 11).

Campbell thought that there really are *not* many different religions. All religions and belief systems are simply variations of the same *mythic motifs*. The famous psychologist, Carl Jung referred to this idea as the "archetype of the collective unconscious."

Campbell felt that when… "the poetry of myth is interpreted as biography, history or science, it is killed." He felt that Christianity, Mohammedanism, and Judaism were the worst offenders in this regard, and bigotry was the result. (*The Hero With A Thousand Faces*, p. 249, 258, 259).

With our technology and mass communication mediums, our world is shrinking to a global community. Campbell foresaw a global Spirituality, or one-world view of religion, which he believed to be absolutely essential if we are ever to overcome extreme fundamental-

110

ism and nationalism. He felt that we would never have freedom from war and bloodshed until we recognize that it is our shared experience (myth) which shapes all belief systems.

There are some interesting anomalies that Campbell noted very briefly. He noticed that although the snake is a sacred creature in most cultures and given a positive interpretation, this is not so in the Bible. He called it an interesting twist. And he found the Hebrew teaching that there is only one God, to be unique, and something he did not understand.

In his book *The Inner Reaches of Outer Space,* Campbell noted that Kundalini yoga is not a game of "as if" or make believe, "… but an actual experience of psychological absorption in a metaphysical ground of some kind …" (p. 102). And in *The Power of Myth,* Campbell said, "Three or four times I've seen what appear to be magical effects occur; men and women of power can do things that you wouldn't think possible…" (p. 142).

In the same book, Campbell summarized his findings with this statement, "…we do know that burials always involve the idea of the continued life beyond the visible one, of a plane of being that is behind the visible plane, and that is somehow supportive of the visible one to which we have to relate. I would say that is the basic theme of all mythology—that there is an invisible plane supporting the visible one" (p. 71).

Do you see now why I was excited about Randy Morrison's experience with the spirit boats and people? He was experiencing the *mythic motif* of the world, and perpetuating it, even if he didn't understand what was going on.

There is a common idea today that we all have a destiny and we each must follow our calling. Some higher power will lead us, or we will find our "way" by reaching deep within. This higher power, no matter what we call it, is in reality, the same power or god for all of us. All of us will wind up at the same place in the end and all paths lead to that place. Joseph Campbell would say that you must find your path and follow it, and this is the inner longing of every person. You can make your own spirituality and find your own religion.

But what if Joseph Campbell is wrong? If all religions are simply variations of the same mythic motifs, then one could simply pick whatever philosophy works for him. But if there is a world-view that is *radically* different, would it not be worth examining?

The world's philosophies and teachings are so intertwined and related, that you would almost think that at the core level, there is one system of thought. But actually, there are two. The language may be similar; but the philosophies could not be more opposite and opposed! What I have to say next may be disturbing for some, but I hope it will be interesting for all.

Chapter 42

Star Wars

Finding my "path," as Joseph Campbell puts it, has been sort of a difficult experience. I was raised in a Christian tradition, and when young, simply assumed a lot of things. Life was simple, and fairly black and white. In the 8th grade I took a correspondence course in Greek mythology/literature. It was then that I began to question the Bible stories I had been taught. The story of the great flood, for example, is perhaps the most widely told story in the world. Why didn't we refer to the Bible version as *Hebrew* mythology, I wondered? Then came my introduction to the theory of evolution. In college I decided the time had come to find out for myself, once and for all, whether or not there was a supreme Creator-God. I may tell what happened, later.

Most people have heard something of the terrible Biblical number 666, which plays a significant part at the end of earth's history. This is an ancient astrological number that comes from Babylon. For those who like mind puzzles, consider this: The numbers 1, 6, 12, 36,111, and 666 were sacred numbers. The letter S derived from a pictograph of a cobra erected in its striking position. The hissing sound represented the voice. Snake, serpent, Satan and sun were all interwoven.

The serpent in its striking and coiled position formed the letter S and the number 6. The number 666 was sometimes written as SSS.

Now, add the numbers 1 through 36 and see what you get. If you were to take an astrological chart from the Berlin museum, you would find the numbers 1-36 all mixed up, but never repeating, and arranged in 6 horizontal rows and 6 vertical columns. Add the numbers across, and then add them up or multiply by 6. Add them vertically and do the same. Add them crosswise.

06 32 03 34 35 01	01 32 34 03 35 06
07 11 27 28 08 30	30 08 27 28 11 07
19 14 16 15 23 24	20 24 15 16 13 23
18 20 22 21 17 13	19 17 21 22 18 14
25 29 10 09 26 12	10 26 12 09 29 25
36 05 33 04 02 31	31 04 02 33 05 36

It may be that the cross is hidden in these charts. The *cross* is associated with serpent and sun, and has always represented the link between heaven and earth and life-after-death ideas. Thus, the cross is often depicted within a solar disk. The Egyptian ankh and Hitler's swastika are variations of the cross, which comes from Tammuz, the reincarnated and ancient Nimrod sun god. Another form of the cross is found in the three-pronged trident (666) source of the idea for the devil's pitchfork.

The Bible tells of a tree of life from which Adam and Eve were allowed to eat. They were not allowed to eat of the tree of knowledge of good and evil. It was here that Eve met the serpent and was promised a different kind of wisdom and assured that she would not die. Thereafter they were blocked from the tree of life.

After the flood, Nimrod founded the city of Babylon and was responsible for a belief system that established the tower of Babel. Babylon (Bible version) represented everything rebellious and evil. At the tower, God confounded the language of the people and the teachings spread around the world in the various new tongues. Later, in a major way, the teachings went from the nation of Babylon to Persia to Greece to Rome to us. In Babylon, science and medicine combined real authentic knowledge, with occult knowledge, just like today. The (Hebrew, Jewish, Israelite) version of the story begins with Genesis, the book of beginnings, and ends with Revelation, the book that *reveals* past, present and future. And in this book, it is revealed that time as we know it, is nearly finished.

I once read a book that said the Hebrew people were very clever for having invented a single, universal God who could not be seen. They could have no idols, ate different food, had a different day of worship, kept themselves separate and abhorred most everything about the spiritual life of their neighbors. At least that's the way it was sometimes; an awful lot of other times they were unable to maintain their strict standards.

They became known as the nation of Israel after one of their great forefathers, Jacob, had his name changed by God, to "Israel." Through war and assimilation, the nation was reduced to a couple of tribes, with the tribe of Judah becoming the predominant one—hence the name "Jew." The Jews, although a minority, attacked and taken captive many times, have somehow managed to maintain their identity.

Those Jews, who believed that Jesus was their long-awaited Messiah, became known as Christians, because they talked so much about Jesus Christ. Thus, Christianity is really Jewish, begun by thousands of Jews, including many priests (Acts 2:41, 4:4, 6:7). For some reason, the God and Jesus of the Judeo-Christian religion has been picked for special revile and cursing. Have you ever heard anyone angrily use the name "Buddha" or "Krishna" as a swear word? Many do not know or do not care that one of the 10 commandments takes special notice of those who misuse God's name (Ex. 20:7).

The Bible says that God created the first people and also angels and things normally unseen to us (Col. 1:16; Heb. 1, 2). We are involved in a struggle with spiritual forces that are not flesh and blood and we need everything God can give us (Eph. 6:10-18).

This struggle began when one very high angel had everything, but became proud, and was expelled from God's presence and thrown to earth (Eze. 28:11-19). He is a *pretender,* and masquerades as an *angel of light* (2 Cor. 11:14). The name of this high and mighty angel was Lucifer, meaning *light-bearer* or *shining one.* He wanted to be worshipped just like God (Isa. 14:11-17). Jesus spoke of seeing him fall from heaven (Luke 10:18). And he came with many *other* deceiving angels (Rev. 12:9).

Lucifer was and is a super- intelligent, handsome, but *created* being. He, just like Adam and Eve, was created a free moral agent and God has never forced love or respect. He became known as Satan, which means adversary. The Bible also calls him Beelzebub, and a tempter, devil, and deceiver. Jesus called him a murderer and a liar and the father of lies (John 8:44). He and his evil angels are the power behind idolatry and heathen worship systems (1 Cor. 10:19, 20). That is why God said it was an abomination to practice passing- through the fire, divination, astrology, spells, witchcraft, wizardry, communication with familiar spirits or ghosts, or communication with anyone who has died (Deut. 18:10-12).

The names for some of these practices constantly change. Today we might call some of these things names like Ouija (yes, in two languages) crystal ball reading, tarot cards (from which the 52 card deck derived with its 36 numbered cards totaling the mystic number 666 which is also the sum of the jack, queen and king), palm reading, teacup reading, psychic ability, channeling, automatic writing, yoga—the list goes on and on. Many strange healing and unique health techniques would appear to also fall into the Bible's forbidden list.

In Genesis, (the book of beginnings) not only do we find the story of the first people, we also find a strange story of a talking snake. This serpent told Adam and Eve that if they ate of a tree God had said to leave alone, they would not die as He had warned, but would instead be enlightened and be as gods (Gen. 3:1-6).

The snake was cursed to crawl upon its belly—(remember the story told all over the world of the wonderful flying serpent?) Joseph Campbell said the Bible has a twist to the story and it certainly does. But there is more. The Bible also identifies the serpent as a primary symbol for Satan himself, and warns that he leads the whole world

115

astray. It appears that the serpent was just a medium for something much more sinister.

The Bible says, "We know that we are children of God, and that the whole world is under the control of the evil one. We know also that the Son of God has come and has given us understanding, so that we may know him who is true. And we are in him who is true-even in his Son Jesus Christ. He is the true God and eternal life" (1 John 5:19, 20).

If the Bible is simply a part of a world mythology, then the story it tells can be ignored, but if there is any chance that it is something more, then this statement is sobering indeed! "And there was war in heaven. Michael and his angels fought against the dragon, and the dragon and his angels fought back. But he was not strong enough, and they lost their place in heaven. The great dragon was hurled down— that ancient serpent called the devil or Satan, who leads the whole world astray. He was hurled to the earth, and his angels with him" (Rev. 12:7, 9).

Some of what the Bible has to say, steps on toes. But it also reveals that the *whole* world has been deceived. And it is a book for all people. Here's another passage from the *"book that reveals"*: "And I saw three unclean spirits like frogs come out of the mouth of the dragon, and out of the mouth of the beast, and out of the mouth of the false prophet. For they are the spirits of devils, working miracles, which go forth unto the kings of the earth and of the whole world, to gather them to the battle of that great day of God Almighty" (Rev. 16:13, 14).

Perhaps, for interest's sake, we should take a look at death from the Bible's point of view. After all, Jesus said that Satan has been a liar from the beginning, and it was the serpent who said that the first people would not die. And as Joseph Campbell has said, this is the established worldview and the *"basic theme of all mythology."*

116

Chapter 43

Death

The major worldview of death and the predominant Christian view is that there is a part of us that is immortal. But more and more theologians of various denominations are speaking out against this idea. They are telling us that all life and thought ceases at death, no one goes immediately to heaven or hell, and a resurrection is the only hope for any future existence beyond the grave.

A dangerous belief has rapidly infiltrated the whole world. Mythologist, Joseph Campbell, was absolutely right when he defined the basic theme of all mythology as a belief in a spirit world and a life beyond the grave.

Jesus said there are only two paths; one is wide with many travelers, but the other that leads to life is narrow and very few find it (Matt. 7:13, 14). Jesus said that He was the truth and the life (John 14:6) and the resurrection and the life (John 11:25). And the apostle Peter added that there was only one name under heaven that could save us (Acts 4:12). In today's world, Jesus is mostly considered to be just one of many important ways to truth, or a liar.

According to the Bible, only God has immortality (1 Tim. 6:16). We can seek for it and it is promised (Rom. 2:7) but only at Christ's coming (1 Cor. 15:53, 54). Death is not a joyous new experience but rather, ***the last enemy to be destroyed!*** (1 Cor. 15:26).

A future resurrection is the hope of all Christians. Without a bodily resurrection, there is no life after death. Paul points out that our only hope lies in Christ and his promise of future life. "And if Christ be not raised, your faith is vain; ye are yet in your sins. Then they also which are fallen asleep in Christ are perished" (1 Cor. 15:17, 18). The most famous of all Bible promises says, "For God so loved the world, that he gave his only begotten Son, that whosoever believeth in him should not *perish*, but have everlasting life" (John 3:16).

In the Bible, the Hebrew "ruach" and the Greek "pneuma" are often translated as spirit, but consciousness is not attributed to these words *after death.* A living *soul* or *being* (person) is composed of body and "breath of life" (Gen. 2:7). At death this breath or "life force" returns to God who gave us life and the opposite occurs—death of the whole person; the soul ceases to exist (Eccl. 12:7).

The "spirit" or "life-principle" obviously must reside with the Creator-God. The life-principle of wicked men, righteous men and even animals, returns to God (Eccl. 3:19, 20). The NIV puts Job 27:3, 4 this way, "as long as I have life within me, the breath of God in my nostrils, my lips will not speak wickedness, and my tongue will utter no deceit. The same verse in the KJV says, "all the while my breath is in me, and the spirit of God is in my nostrils…"

It takes both body and spirit (life) to produce thought, just as it takes a computer plus electricity to produce function. Similarly, nails and boards can make a box, but separate them, and the box disappears.

Death is creation in reverse. The soul is the whole functioning person; all souls belong to God, and souls can die (Gen. 2:7; Eze. 18:4). At death we do not reincarnate, or become spirits or angels. We do not go to heaven or hell; we go to sleep! Over and over again the Bible refers to death as a sleep, because it is temporary until the resurrection. All will rise again to give answer to the Creator (John 5:28, 29; Rom. 14:10-12).

Death is a rest, a perfect sleep of non-existence. Jesus, before raising his friend Lazarus from the dead, spoke of him as sleeping. Then he explained, "Lazarus is dead" (John 11:11-14).

Do people go to heaven when they die?

"By the sweat of your brow you will eat your food until you return to the ground, since from it you were taken; for *dust* you are and to *dust* you will return (Gen. 3:19). But man dies and is laid low; he breathes his last and is no more (Job 14:12). When you hide your face, they are terrified; when you take away their breath, they die and return to the dust (Ps. 104:29). All go to the same place; all come from dust and to dust all return (Eccl. 3:20). Brothers, I can tell you confidently that the patriarch David died and was buried, and his tomb is here to this day. For David did not ascend to heaven, and yet he said, "The Lord said to my Lord: Sit at my right hand" (Acts 2:29, 34). But man dies and is laid low, he breathes his last and is no more. So man lies down and does not rise; till the heavens are no more, men will not awake or be roused from their *sleep* (Job 14:10, 12). But Christ has indeed been raised from the dead, the firstfruits of those who have fallen *asleep*. But each in his own turn; Christ, the firstfruits; then, when he comes, those who belong to him (1 Cor. 15:20, 23). Martha answered, "I know he will rise again in the *resurrection at the last day*" (John 11:24).

Do the dead know anything?

"If his sons are honoured, he does not know it; if they are brought low he does not see it" (Job 14:21). "No one remembers you when he is dead. Who praises you from the grave?" (Ps. 6:5). "His breath goeth forth, he returns to his earth; in that very day his thoughts perish" (Ps. 146:4). "For the living know that they will die, but the dead know nothing; they have no further reward, and even the memory of them is forgotten" (Eccl. 9:5). "For the grave cannot praise you, death cannot sing your praise; those who go down to the pit cannot hope for your faithfulness. The living, the living, they praise you, as I am doing today" (Isa. 38:18, 19).

Can the dead communicate with the living?

"So man lies down and does not rise; till the heavens are no more, men will not awake or be roused from their sleep" (Job 14:12). "It is not the dead who praise the Lord, those who go down into silence" (Ps. 115:17). "Their love, their hate and their jealousy have long since vanished; never again will they have a part in anything that happens under the sun. Whatever your hand finds to do, do it with all your might, for in the grave where you are going, there is neither working, nor planning nor knowledge nor wisdom" (Eccl. 9:6, 10). "As a cloud vanishes and is gone, so he who goes down to the grave does not return. He will never come to his house again; his place will know him no more" (Job 7:9, 10).

If it is not the dead, then who are the spirits and voices that people talk to?

119

"But I am afraid just as Eve was deceived by the serpent's cunning, your minds may somehow be led astray from your sincere and pure devotion to Christ. For if someone comes to you and preaches a Jesus other than the Jesus we preached or if you receive a different spirit from the one you received, or a different gospel from the one you accepted you put up with it easily enough" (2 Cor. 11:3, 4). "The great dragon was hurled down—that ancient serpent called the devil, or Satan, who leads the whole world astray. He was hurled to the earth, and his angels with him" (Rev. 12:9). "And no wonder, for Satan himself masquerades as an angel of light" (2 Cor. 11:14). "Let no one be found among you who sacrifices his son or daughter in the fire, who practices divination or sorcery, interprets omens, engages in witchcraft or casts spells, or who is a medium or spiritualist or who consults the dead" (Deut. 18:10, 11). "The Spirit clearly says that in later times some will abandon the faith and follow deceiving spirits and things taught by demons" (1 Tim. 4:1). "Do not turn to mediums or seek out spiritualists, for you will be defiled by them. I am the Lord your God" (Lev. 19:31). "For false Christs and false prophets will appear and perform great signs and miracles to deceive even the elect—if that were possible" (Matt. 24:24). "They are spirits of demons performing miraculous signs, and they go out to the kings of the whole world, to gather them for the battle on the great day of God Almighty" (Rev.16: 14). "For our struggle is not against flesh and blood, but against the rulers, against authorities, against the powers of this dark world and against the spiritual forces of evil in the heavenly realms" (Eph. 6:1).

I am going to suggest that the world and mythological view (especially Greek mythology) has had a profound impact on us, even those of us who are Christians. The dualistic idea of a spirit living in a body has infiltrated us too. And with that idea comes awful possibilities for deception. And one more thing—if what I have presented from the Bible is true, then there is no-one suffering in the fires of hell right now. Dante could have written about something more uplifting.

The definition of love is that "God is love" (1 John 4:8, 16). How can this God torture an unbeliever forever and ever throughout the ceaseless ages of eternity? Although the hot fire has been used to gain converts, this teaching has actually produced more hatred for God than any other teaching. And it comes from the same mythology that gives us our ideas regarding death.

I am surprised at how many Christians seem to prefer the always-burning, eternal, and everlasting fires of hell. There are some verses that almost seem to read that way but there are simple explanations. The word "gospel" means "*good news*" and I think the gospel of Jesus is literally overflowing with good news! *

For free information on this subject and the subject of hell, visit www.amazingfacts.org, www.Bibleuniverse.com, or www.3abn.org

An excellent book is one called *Living Lies About Death And The Hereafter* by Henry Feyerabend. Find it on the internet, at any Adventist Book Center, or through TEACH Services, who published this book.

A scholarly study is a book called *Immortality or Resurrection?* by Dr. Samuele Bacchiocchi. It can be found similarly or by contacting www.biblicalperspectives.com or by calling 269-471-2915

Chapter 44

Zeballos

Ron Johnston is a fishing buddy who belongs to no church as yet. But he read some books about prayer and the supernatural, by a man named Roger Morneau. Then Ron told me that he did not believe the stories.

Shortly thereafter Ron left the boat, bought a big truck and hauled from Vancouver to Arizona. One day, at a truck stop, Ron mentioned this author to another trucker. The truck driver surprised him by saying that he knew Roger Morneau and had attended his church. Then he added, "Everyone knows that when Roger prays, things happen."

Trucks are moving all across North America and Ron meets the one trucker who knows Roger. This trucker added that he was collecting news articles about Roger's recent death. Ron's mouth fell open and he could hardly wait to tell me about the experience. I asked Ron if he thought the whole encounter was just by chance and he said that he had been thinking about that.

Ron was still marveling about this "chance" encounter, when we later wound up in Zeballos for the herring fishery. Zeballos is a little fishing and logging town on the west coast of Vancouver Island. It is quite popular with tourists and was once a thriving gold mining town. There are still some reminders of the wild, old mining days.

There is a picturesque and rustic, old hotel. A waitress told us the hotel was haunted, which made the place more interesting for tourists. She said that during the gold rush days, a Chinese lady named Susie had worked there as a maid, and died. She sometimes threw the laundry around and turned the TV on and off to make her presence known from the spirit world. This waitress had personally experienced these things but chuckled about them.

I was curious about her story and wanted more verification. I was told where the owner of the hotel could be found and that I would be sure to recognize him. He was described as looking like a "biker-type" with a full beard down to his chest. Sure enough, he was an interesting-looking character and proved to have an interesting tale.

He was sorting bills and counting money. He did not even look up when I asked about the reports of a spirit in the hotel. He said he did not believe in spirits but I let him know that I did and that I had some personal experience with such. Then his attitude suddenly changed, and without explaining why, he told me to go and push a swinging bar door that separated the public area from the serving quarters behind the counter. He kept on doing what he was doing.

I checked out the old door which had worn the carpet away with all the swinging of many years. It sagged on its hinges and had to be pushed hard or lifted to get it to open. The man said, "It's hard to move isn't it?" When I agreed, he continued, "When this place is really hoppin, that door is swingin wildly back and forth, all by itself." Then he explained the spirit connection, "There's two of em, but they're perfectly harmless." Since he made no effort to continue the conversation, I let myself out.

The waitress believed in re-incarnation and had had her future foretold by a psychic. Her children were very interested in experiences of people who had supposedly died and come back to life. I tried to share some Bible information with her but she got too worked up and excited. I decided the timing wasn't right and kept the material on the boat.

The herring wouldn't spawn. Only one other time in history was this known to have happened. Further up the coast, Prince Rupert was ready for fishing and the fishermen who were licensed for both areas, panicked. There was a mad scramble and Ron and I wound up rushing north. Some other fishermen caught a ride with us and along the way, asked about our beliefs. I shared some things from the Bible and told some personal answer-to-prayer stories.

A young fellow listened quietly and said not a word. But the next morning Ron shared his truck story and offered Roger's book *The Incredible Power of Prayer*. Then our visitor said, "It's not by chance that I'm on this boat." He had prayed that if there was a God in heaven that he might find Him. His mother had warned him not to pray that prayer unless he meant it.

For three weeks he had been waiting in Zeballos and he had been thinking that he should do something about his question. Then he met us. His head was spinning. I gave him the material the other lady had not been ready for. Steve *was* ready.

On my return home, and several weeks later, I prayed for guidance (with some church friends) and decided that at some point, I would drive to Zeballos. One day I was returning home from a trip to Campbell River. On the spur of the moment I decided to make the 1 hr. trip each way, into the little community, over a rough gravel road and in pouring rain. I talked to God along the way and told him how silly I felt. But I wanted a story that would show His care and power.

I did not know the woman's name or where she lived. I knew only that she had previously worked part-time at the Zeballos Hotel. I drove through the community and did not see her. I stopped at the Hotel but the restaurant was closed. I could see some people inside and thought I would get their attention and describe the lady to them. Maybe they would know something. I bowed my head and prayed. When I looked up, the closed sign had been changed; the restaurant was now open.

I walked in and the lady I wanted to see was sitting at a table. She recognized me and remembered my name. When she asked me why I was there I told her the truth. I had been thinking about our previous conversation.

This time I gave her some excellent material with my phone number. The Bible teaches that the dead do not return and that our thoughts cease at death, until the resurrection. Evil spirits are increasingly seeking to deceive us and even impersonate people who have died.

She thanked me and promised to read the material the next day on her way out of Zeballos. She was leaving the community and her goods had already been moved. She would not have a phone in her new residence. That day was her last day in Zeballos and my final opportunity to talk to her. It was almost as if she had been waiting for me.

I cannot forget a strange question Steve had for me, while on the boat. He asked, "Do you have a sense of urgency?" For some reason that he could not explain, he had a driving sense of urgency. And I must admit - increasingly - so do I.

Chapter 45

Back to That Elusive Great Ape

One of the definitions for the word "ape" is a *mimic* or *imitator*. And what often startles people who have encountered a Sasquatch is the uncanny way it seems to be almost human but also somewhat ethereal. It walks like us, turns its head like we do, communicates and yet always seems just out of reach. Various Indian tribes believe it to exist in a spiritual dimension and they say that Sasquatch is seen only when it wants to be seen. And often, encounters include an irrational sense of fear.

Variations of the story shift around the world. And although this elusive creature seems to exhibit certain ape-like characteristics (stone throwing, limb breaking, tree twisting etc.) it also exhibits a strength that is difficult to comprehend. Massive boulders moved or thrown and trees that are snapped, twisted or bent, are among the many stories told.

A friend who heard that I had some Sasquatch stories wanted my opinion on his experience. He and another man had been hunting a remote mountain valley in Oregon, he said, and as they drove their jeep along an old overgrown logging road they encountered trees freshly twisted and broken, crossing their path. As they proceeded, the size of the trees and the quantity became larger and larger until they could no longer go forward. It was very obvious that something wanted them out of the area.

One tree had all the limbs pulled out (not snapped off) up to about 9 feet. In one place all the trees in a circle had been dropped on the trail and there were fir trees snapped over up to 8 inches in diameter. A depression area for a bed was found and beside the bed was a very large human-like footprint. There was a strong foul musk odor.

The lateness of the afternoon, coupled with a sense of foreboding, made them very uneasy. They could account for no living creature that could create the kind of havoc that they were witnessing. The other hunter shocked my friend by suddenly exclaiming that they were intruding upon a Sasquatch family and that it was time to exit the area.

I remember camping many years ago at the back of Long Lake in Smith Inlet. This was an ancient traditional salmon harvesting and smoking area for the Gwa'Sala Indian people. Periodically throughout the night my rest was disturbed by loud cracks that sounded for all the world like large limbs being broken. At the time I had no way to account for the strange phenomenon.

I went to see Dr. John Bindernagel who is working on his second Sasquatch book. He first became interested while in his third year of University and has since personally collected some 150 stories. As a biologist who wants to be taken credibly, he is most interested in evidence that appears to be solidly entrenched in the physical realm. He has found footprints and made his own casts. It is the large human-like footprints noted by many enthusiasts and researchers that produced the name "Bigfoot."

Bindernagel says that other physical evidence includes tree and branch breaking, rock throwing, and a terrible smell that is so often reported of Sasquatch encounters. He says that these characteristics are also distinctive of big apes. And the scores of descriptions regarding appearance, type of walk, etc. are consistent. Dr. Bindernagel believes the Sasquatch to be an intelligent, elusive, mostly nocturnal big ape.

I would once have paid no attention to any of it; but I must admit that I have gone from a laughing skeptic to a believer—of—sorts. I know the people who have shared their stories. They are not all a bunch of liars and I also know that they have no reason to be made a laughing - stock or the brunt of hilarious jokes. I know that they experienced something strange but unlike Bindernagel, I am not discounting the supernatural element. I think perhaps we need to listen to that aspect of what the Native people have been telling us.

In the book *Indian Healing* researcher Wolfgang Jilek writes of the resurgence of Shamanic Ceremonialism in the Pacific Northwest. It is filled with stories and personal experiences that defy normal explanation. It is a book that verifies much of what I have written previously. And while I do not deny the reality of Sasquatch encounters, I think that the explanation for such lies squarely within the realm of spirits, serpents and dragons.

There are stories of footprints that disappear. One person saw a Sasquatch standing in front of the Bighouse in Alert Bay—an island community and hardly a forest. My American friend, Mark, found that some Natives believe the Sasquatch to exist in an intermediate state between the living and the dead.

"The people of Nepal call it a "*rakshasa*" which is Sanskrit for "demon." According to them, stories of its existence date back to the fourth-century BCE; references to the Yeti are found in a poem called 'Rama and Sita.' It has regularly been sighted since 1832. Yeti means "magical creature." The name 'The Abominable Snowman' however, was given to it by western newspapers who wanted to give their readers the feeling of terror which the creature supposedly causes in the valleys, crevices and glaciers of the Himalayas" (Internet Encyclopedia of Mythology).

I am not looking for the elusive ape. The joke I played on my wife is not so funny when you consider that someone much bigger may be playing with all of us. He is the master trickster, story-teller and liar. If it suits his purposes he will appear as an angel of light. He likes to be worshipped as God. Jesus said that he was a murderer, a liar and the father of lies. He used a serpent in the beginning and the serpent has become his insignia. The game he plays is for keeps.

One man told of a night encounter just outside his house. He came face to face with a large ape-like creature and then the creature was suddenly looking down on him from a 6-foot-high woodpile. It didn't really jump and it didn't float —it was suddenly just there, above him, and it freaked him badly.

He was overcome with a terrifying sense of fear and could not erase from his memory, the picture of the creature's eyes—which glowed red in the dark. And for a long time he could not go outside his home after nightfall.

I took the opportunity to tell him about Lucifer, the beautiful created angel who rebelled against his Creator and is now known as Satan. I told him about the Garden of Eden and the talking snake who told the first lie. And we talked about Jesus who came to give us freedom from fear and hope for the future. We can know him personally and knowing him is as opposite from the darkness and fear of Satan as you can get.

Jesus said that he came to set the captives free and that he was the light of the world. And he said that we could know the truth and that the truth would set us free (John 8:32). That is why missionaries go around the world offering a new life now and eternal life in a better world to come.

The Bible says, "And ye shall seek me, and find me, when ye shall search for me with all your heart" (Jer. 29:13). For an earnest seeker the promise is sure and there are no exceptions.

Chapter 46

My Crisis of Faith

My crisis of faith came when I hit college, and it was Christians who shook me up. I began looking at people; it seemed like a lot of them did not live what they believed. And I completely forgot how God had helped me in the past.

I decided that many people must not believe in a real, personal God. And I began to wonder why I believed in the existence of someone I had never seen and whose voice I had never literally heard. I determined to do some research and to live my life accordingly.

I began to read the Bible critically and I thought I found all kinds of discrepancies. But later reading produced answers to many of my questions and I came to the conclusion that the book had to have been produced under the direction of a mind much greater than my own.

I was impressed with the accuracy of prophecy and I noted that the people, cities and places it mentions, actually existed. I decided that it could not be both mythology and fact or it would lose all relevance and significance.

During my research on water witching, I had come across a strange book called *Psychic Discoveries Behind the Iron Curtain*. I found that it raised more questions than answers in its efforts to explain the paranormal. I became increasingly convinced that the Bible contained the answers to our world's perplexing questions. And some of those answers were so disturbing and unorthodox that I wondered how a person could verbalize them even if they were true.

The Bible unconditionally promises that the person who searches with all his heart will find God. I began to feel a great sense of peace and assurance.

I had previously thought that if God did exist, He was unfair. I had not asked to be born and I had no power over my circumstances or struggle to find meaning. But I found that while one man (Adam) produced this mess, another man (Jesus) offered the free gift of salvation and righteousness. I had not asked for either and Jesus not only forgives; He also cleanses.

I was reading my Bible one day when I heard some friends coming. Instead of quickly putting it aside as I usually did, I kept it open. And the thing I had feared, happened. One of my friends sneered, "Watcha doing McGill? Reading your Bible?"

Later, that same friend very deliberately plunked his empty beer bottle down beside my desk and walked out. Linda (now my wife) was the last person to talk to him. It was late, he was a bit inebriated and she impatiently told him to take a shower and go to bed.

He did go down to the dorm's bath area where he turned all the showers on full blast and hot. It produced a steam effect and unfortunately, he passed out. When he was discovered in the morning, he was unrecognizable. And I was asked to be one of his pallbearers.

Linda felt bad for having been impatient with him and I felt bad for having been embarrassed about my Bible reading. That book probably could have helped him immensely.

Fear of ridicule can produce disastrous results, and I have been a slow learner.

Eventually, I took a year off from school and went logging. I avoided the subject of religion but one day the hook-tender asked me some very pointed and important questions in the area of parapsychology and the supernatural. He specifically mentioned the "Psychic Discoveries" book that I had also read. He tried to appear casual but I sensed that he was intensely concerned.

I have wondered since, if my vague answer contributed to his suicide. He had picked a private moment to talk to me but I still worried that he might tell the other men. So I answered, "Who knows for sure what the human mind is capable of?"

I wanted to tell him about the Garden of Eden, Adam and Eve, and the very first lie. And I wanted to tell him about Lucifer, now called Satan, who has been deceiving us ever since and is concerned only with our destruction. Instead, I decided that I would talk to him again, at a more convenient time. But he committed suicide shortly after and I was plagued with remorse.

It was 12 years later that I was a little braver (but not much) and I had been asked to conduct a public seminar dealing with the prophetic books of Daniel and Revelation. We had covered a subject entitled, "The Dragon of Antiquity" and we were about to deal with some of the great lies that have been perpetrated upon the world.

On a whim, I decided to talk privately, to the Creator-God who likes to be called "Our Father." I told Him that I would be willing to talk to the wife of the man who had died many years earlier. And although I did not know the woman, I asked that God would somehow arrange the meeting.

The next day I was doing some research in the library and museum. I was standing in the museum when the receptionist, who had been talking to another woman about fortune telling, asked me what I thought about the subject. I had been wondering if I should say something but I also had the impression that I should wait and watch.

I showed them, from the books that I had, what the ancients had believed about some of these things. And I asked if they had visited the Egyptian exhibit at the Vancouver World's Fair and seen the winged serpent on the coffin, representing the immortality of the soul.

The lady who had been visiting with the receptionist became more and more excited, until she exclaimed, "It's really true!" Then she described how a spirit, claiming to be a long departed relative, had come to be her guide and protector. When he was near, she experienced wonderful warmth. Sometimes she actually felt a physical touch to her shoulder.

She received advice regarding foods to eat for her health and she was told which chemicals to use in her commercial gardening business. She was told that there was no heaven or hell and that everyone goes to the same place and that there was nothing to fear. She also experienced automatic writing.

Her husband refused to admit that these things were happening, she said, until they both saw a black cat materialize in their living room. Then he made her promise never to tell anyone for fear that their sanity might be questioned. I knew that I had the right woman when she mentioned her husband's name. And I finally understood why he had asked his questions so carefully.

When I explained my former connection to her husband, she was surprised and shocked. I explained my belief that there is no existence beyond the grave, until the resurrection, even though deceiving spirits would have us believe otherwise. And I said that any spirit's claim to the contrary, was an automatic indication of a demonic encounter.

I invited both women to the next day's seminar which would delve deeper into the subject. Neither of them attended but the experience helped me to teach with more conviction and urgency. I thought I had known what I believed but I remember saying to myself, "It's really true!"

One night, about three months later, I couldn't sleep and I found myself thinking that the woman I had talked to deserved to know how it was that she had come to meet me and that it had not been an accident. Since I wasn't sleeping anyway, I decided to write a letter and tell my story, leading up to my request that God would bring about a meeting if He wished it.

I was going to mail the letter but thought that maybe I should try just one time to physically deliver it. I was afraid that if I mailed it I might never know the outcome. And I realized that malevolent spirit beings might try to frustrate my plans. I told the Lord that I would go by her house on the way to the Post Office. I sort of hoped that she would not be home.

She was home but she seemed not to recognize me. I realized that she had only met me once and that it had been some 3 months prior. I felt awkward and stumbled around a bit before coming to the point. "Do you remember our conversation in the museum," I asked? Her answer shocked me. "Yes I do," she replied, "and I've been wondering how we came to have that conversation." "That's why I'm here," I said, and I handed her the letter.

I told her that I would stop by later to see if she wanted to talk further. She did want to talk and she had many questions. She also filled me in on some history. Yoga, automatic writing and a Ouija board had all been a part of her past.

I told her what I knew and explained that God knows when we are innocently deceived and gives opportunity for reflection in a variety of ways. Knowledge can be fulfilling but it also brings responsibility. There was no laughing.

She said that if it was indeed true that there was a being called Satan and that if he and his angels had been around for thousands of years gaining knowledge about us, then he would have an amazing advantage. And to claim life beyond the grave would be the ultimate deception.

My purpose in telling some of these stories is to raise the realization that the Bible is still relevant for us today. Most people, including Christians, have never actually read it through for themselves, even once. And the Bible's story of salvation is the greatest story ever told.

Chapter 47

Travellers

At this time of year it seems as if all nature is on the move. The salmon are traveling to their place of origin—in many cases, a journey that covers thousands of miles. Even some of the little pink salmon that pass Port Hardy still have hundreds of miles to travel up the mighty Frazer before they enter small tributary streams.

Gray whales should start showing up pretty soon as they return to Mexico for the winter. And towards the end of August some really strange "deadheads" show up.

If you should see a big log (deadhead) protruding from the water that somehow begins to look more and more weird as you approach, and if it suddenly disappears or shocks you with an ugly looking face, it is probably an elephant seal. These animals like to enjoy the sunshine on quiet, fall days and the odd one can be spotted sometimes out towards Pine Island.

They are very large creatures that look somewhat similar to a walrus and they have ugly heads and thick elephant-like trunks—hence the name "elephant seal."

This is the time of year when nature parades the progeny of the short summer season and young creatures are returning with their families to their winter homes. I know that the fall season has arrived when flocks of phalaropes pass the boats.

These little sandpiper-like birds often travel in large groups but unlike the little shore pipers, these birds land on the water and spin around, dipping and bobbing, as they search for tidbits from the sea. And as they journey to the southern hemisphere, they are always on the lookout for dangerous falcons swooping down from above.

As we were returning from a halibut trip one fall night, we got caught in a nasty storm. We nailed plywood over some of the windows and flipped the switch to a large working light that illuminated the area in front of the boat.

A flock of pine grosbeaks was flying with us—way out there in the middle of the ocean. These are land birds of the forests and must have been blown off course. All night these little birds chattered, as they flew in the comforting beam of light, and just in front of the boat. When daylight arrived, and still with no land anywhere in sight, they veered off to go –who –knows –where. But they seemed to know what they were doing.

I marvel at things like that and I marvel that a little hummingbird can travel 500 miles non-stop across the Gulf of Mexico. The ruby-throated hummingbird travels as far as 5,000 miles on its migration flight.

Swallows use some kind of built-in timer to return to Capistrano at exactly the same time each year. And barn swallows will travel 9,000 miles to Argentina. But the arctic tern flies from the north to the south, a distance of 14,000 miles. Astounding.

Higher, higher,
Smaller, smaller,
Softly, so softly,
On cushioned tips,

Freedom's symbol,
Now a speck,
Into dimensions unknown,
Oh that **I** could simply—
Glide away.

Drifting, drifting,
Floating, floating,
Upwards and onwards
Without a glance...

Far from this world,
Not a care,
Rushing away from it all,
Oh that **I** could simply—
Glide away.

Chapter 48

Phenomenal Navigation

The Arctic tern takes all records for migration and navigation distance. The first nest found was only 7 ½ degrees from the North Pole. But a few months after the young are grown, these terns will be found in the Antarctic, 11,000 miles removed from their nesting site.

The homing and navigation ability seems to be inherited. For example, cuckoos, though not raised by their parents, have no problem migrating on their own. Likewise, cowbirds lay their eggs in other bird's nests. Nevertheless, the young know what cowbirds are supposed to do.

As a mariner, there have been times when the fog obscured all visibility beyond a few yards of the boat. And yet, when I raised my eyes from intense concentration on the radar screen, I would see ocean birds (murres and auklets) speeding past me and briefly appearing out of the mist. Since they carried little fish in their bills, it was obvious that they were returning to their homes and families—on an island somewhere, and they knew exactly how to get there.

In experiments performed with starlings, when the young were removed from their nests they migrated parallel to the direction they should have taken. The adults, however, correctly set off to their previous wintering grounds (Oscar Heinroth and Katharina Heinroth, *The Birds*, p. 172).

Similarly, German storks taken to a different section of that country, set off in an easterly direction, the correct direction from their old home, but not from the new area (Gertrud Hess, *The Bird: Its Life and Structure*, p. 40).

Another interesting case concerned mallard eggs shipped from England, where the species does not migrate, to Finland where they do. Of 62 birds, all migrated. Some were shot in Yugoslavia and France; the others returned the next year to Finland (Joseph Hickey, *Guide to Bird Watching*, pp. 42, 43).

Some birds appear to travel by the sun and they can become confused in overcast weather. The timing of their migration is triggered by the sun's inclined angle, which varies from pole to pole and season to season.

Some of the smaller birds, which migrate at night for protection, seem to navigate by the stars. This is the case with garden warblers. They can get their bearings from the stars even when raised indoors away from natural surroundings. These same birds become confused when clouds cover the sky (*The Birds*, pp. 173, 174).

Ornithologist, George Wallace says, "Of the various views that purport to explain direction-finding in birds—recognition of landmarks, detection of magnetic fields, retracing ability, and various centers in the ear or eye—some sort of visual orientation, perhaps aided in some cases by an actual or inherited memory of routes, seems to be the most satisfactory answer. And, as in the case of 'causes of migration,' it seems unlikely that there is any single, workable hypothesis that explains direction finding in all birds, as different birds solve the various problems involved in different ways" (*An Introduction to Ornithology*, p. 234).

We know that whales use under-water sonar and bats use echolocation to navigate and find prey. Salmon use an extremely fine-tuned sense of smell as a part of their homing technique. And once again, I say—astounding.

The geese flew over today,
I heard their mixed-up bugling from on high,
And once again a chilly, tingling, finger...
Touched my spine,
And lifted me - until my spirit filled the sky.

A little boy stopped his raking,
And questioning, tipped his head,
I wondered what thoughts he thought,
Perhaps, already, the flock *he* led.

My fat neighbor sitting in the lawn chair,
Stopped his guzzling, forgot his beer,
Shook his head and loftily informed me,
That almost, my son, winter was here.

I felt a strange but happy loneliness,
And after the prediction, my loneliness increased,
While my spirit continued to expand, higher and higher,
Until I was lost—up there—with the geese.

I could not help but wonder where they went,
How did they know what my fat neighbor knew?
They neither told me nor seemed to care,
But forgot the past, and onward, flew.

Chapter 49

Tony's Story

Tony and Hanny Platen owned an Insurance Agency and delicatessen for many years in Port Alice. But in the summer of 1945, Tony was a 15-year-old boy in war-torn Germany and had been sent on a desperate mission to see if his stepmother and 3 sisters were still alive.

The war had just ended and his Grandmother had asked him to travel from English-occupied Lower Rhineland, to American-occupied Leipzig. Freight trains were crowded with refugees and many people walked. By train, today, the trip would take less than 8 hours but it took Tony many days. He found his family well, but his father was a prisoner of war in Siberia and did not return until 1952.

Then Tony began walking south to Munich, where his mother and her new husband lived. He had to take the news to family and relatives and seek to find out who was alive and who was dead. He slept beside the road at night and sometimes found fruit in local gardens; other times he knocked on doors to beg for bread.

Many days later he arrived, tired and dirty (he had not changed his clothes since leaving Leipzig) at the little town of Blankenstein on the River Saale. He saw that hundreds of people, including many mothers with small children, were just sitting and many were crying.

An elderly man noticed that Tony was young and alone, and told him that he would not be able to travel to Munich or cross the river. The Russians had arrived from the east a week earlier and the Americans had moved across the river, which was now the new border. The kind gentleman took Tony to his "Gasthaus" (Guesthouse) and let him have food, a bath and a good sleep.

Tony learned that many people had been shot while trying to cross the river at night. When he returned the next day, he found the same people still sitting, but the Russian guard was momentarily distracted as he stood in a shelter, talking on the phone, and his back was turned.

Tony inched past the guard and stepped onto the bridge. Then he glanced back at the soldier and then across to the American side. He noticed the Americans making motions for him to proceed, so he kept walking for about 60 meters, until he heard a shout.

The angry Russian guard had his machine gun aimed and was motioning for him to return. When Tony looked to the Americans, he saw that they also had their guns drawn. But their guns were pointing past him and at the Russian, and they were making motions for him to keep coming. So that is exactly what he did.

When he reached safety, he heard shooting on the other side, as the guard forced the people away. The Americans let him catch a military train to Munich.

In 1990, Tony took his wife to visit the spot where he had tested fate 45 years earlier. He asked a man who was washing his car, about the old wooden bridge, which was no longer evident. And then the man showed him a part of the old bridge which had been preserved, along with a memorial plate in honor of all the people who had lost their lives while trying to cross that river.

Tony believes that there were many times when God protected him, but this experience of many years ago is one he will never forget. My next story is about a North Island man who played soccer with Hitler, and yes, I mean **Adolf** Hitler!

Tony worked on a chicken farm after the war and received poverty wages. He left for Canada without telling his employer, who was an uncle. It caused a rift and bothered Tony's conscience even though there really had been no other way. Years later he made a special trip back to Germany to make amends. All was forgiven and the family had a great time and was at peace once again. That night - the very night that the situation was resolved - was the same night that his uncle died of a heart attack.

Chapter 50

War's Long Reach

While writing Tony's story, a good friend passed away, who like Tony, had been a youth in Germany while that country was at war. He later established one of British Columbia's largest plumbing companies.

I once asked Reinhold and his wife questions about the war. Reinhold said that he had been spared from active duty because his father's trade was desperately needed to keep the water systems operating. And something I found very interesting was that the French prisoners of war were not locked up in his village as long as they helped with the emergency repairs.

When the Russians arrived, the French thought they had been liberated, but the soldiers disappeared and were never heard from again. The local girls hid and did not tell even their families where they went; raping was rampant.

My friend's wife told about being caught by a drunken officer and she scratched and bit and got away. Earlier in the war, she had been in a bomb shelter and thought that she was the only one left alive after a raid. The effect on her had been devastating.

As we were talking, I suddenly noticed that the woman was gone. After a time she returned, but she had been crying and I learned that she had not discussed the horrors of the war until that moment. I've since found that it is fairly common to lock these kinds of memories away forever.

I recently talked to a North Island man who personally met Adolf Hitler and received a lapel pin from him after his Hitler Youth group played a game of soccer with Hitler. He said that Adolf could run like the dickens (my word) and kick too. In the game he was treated no differently than anyone else.

Hitler had a dual personality. He seemed to enjoy the kids and he would playfully tousle their hair. His visit pleased my friend because the camp was issued new uniforms and boots and the food was specially prepared. For the first time in his life he was able to see and taste a real orange.

Adolf had a dog that would take your arm off if you approached uninvited. There was a code word that would make the dog behave in a normal manner. A special dinner was being served when some sort of bad news reached the Youth camp. Hitler banged his fist on the table and the whole official motorcade left suddenly with their dinner unfinished. The place was charged and tense with spilled soup everywhere.

This man's family was torn by the war. He remembers his older brother bragging after joining a special SS tank training unit. And he remembers his dad being so upset that he gave his brother a beating when he came home. For that, his father could have lost his life.

Some days his dad would tell him to stay away from the barn but once he wandered. For the first time in his life he saw a black man and he was extremely frightened; it was like seeing a ghost. Since there were no blacks in Germany, he knew that the man must have been an American. It was only after the war that he learned the extent to which his father had been involved in the underground.

His own family has never to this day discussed some of these things. But once when his brother had been drinking, he slipped up with some angry words and showed scars from the beatings he received while a prisoner in England. And the beatings were received *after* the war.

This man remembers back before the war, that he wished he could wear a star like the neighbor kids. One day some soldiers gathered him up with his friends and their mother, but she screamed, "No, he's not one of us!" He now says with emotion, "That Jewish mother probably saved my life." He still remembers the rough treatment and bruises that he received when he was thrown, like an animal, into the back of the truck.

I have not experienced war. I am just beginning to understand why my friend does not want his name used or some of his stories told. Whether German, English, Canadian, American or Russian, war is war, and it evidently has a very long reach.

I've heard stories of bombers that literally blackened the sky over Germany. In one case, when resistance was already greatly diminished, a boy counted 1,100 planes flying overhead, non-stop, and in perfect, deadly formation.

Franz Hasel was drafted into the German army at 40 years of age and assigned to Pioneer Company 699, an engineering unit that built bridges on the front lines. Because he was not supportive of Hitler, he was in just as much danger from his own officers, as he was from the enemy.

Deep inside the Ukraine, the SS troops met up with them and Hasel learned of Hitler's "final solution." The Jewish men, women and children of each new community were rounded up, taken to the forest, and shot. Hasel did his best to warn the Jews, but to his surprise, most were murdered because they refused to leave their homes and possessions immediately.

Because Hasel was a Bible student, the men eventually asked him what was going to happen, according to the Bible. Hasel told them how Nebuchadnezzar, about 602 B.C, had dreamed of a great image with a head of gold, breast and arms of silver, belly and thighs of bronze, legs of iron and feet of mixed iron and clay. Then a stone had smashed the feet and the whole image toppled.

The meaning was that successive nations (Medo-Persia, Greece, Rome) would follow Babylon and then Rome would weaken into 10 major divisions. Christ's coming would constitute the next kingdom, represented by the stone that filled the whole earth.

Hasel's commander, who had been a history teacher, was so impressed that he secretly began conserving fuel. The result was that Hasel's unit, which was the deepest into Russia, had just enough fuel to retreat across the River Enns into American-held territory. And Hasel and his commanding officer were among the 7 who survived out of his 1200-man unit.

At special times we pause to remember the horrors of war and those who risked their lives to liberate the people of Europe, including the people of Germany, many of whom became our friends and neighbors.

Franz Hasel's story is told in the book *A Thousand Shall Fall* by Susi Hasel Mundy and published by the Review and Herald Association, Hagerstown, MD 21740.

I held in my hand the lapel pin that gave my friend such special status when he was a boy in the "Hitler Youth." Military men would snap to attention at that time. It gave me a funny feeling to hold the very pin that had been in the hand of Adolf Hitler—one of the most infamous men who ever lived.

Chapter 51

The Feminist

My wife told me that she hated having me for her boss. "No, no, no," I said, "we're partners." "Yeah, right" was her response. "You *always* shout at me." (She overuses that word) "No, no, no," I argued, "It's just all the excitement and noise on the boat. I have to shout to be heard."

I pointed out that the regular crew didn't ever quit and go inside. Since she was known to have done that, it was proof that she was a partner. And I could have pointed out that the others didn't come up to negotiate, or *demand* that it was time to go to bed.

I sometimes noticed various crew persons talking quietly to my partner just before she came to me with some announcement. They pretended innocence while cautiously observing our conversation but they didn't realize that I had been doing the same with them.

My wife wanted personal fulfillment and explored the possibility of further education. She desired a job and income on her own terms. How could I argue with that? Fishing was going to the dogs anyway.

The Feminist

She did it; she obtained employment and went to school at the same time. She obtained her social work degree and then her Masters degree in counseling. But I have a new problem. She has started using the dreaded f-word; yes, she says that she is now a feminist.

My wife assures me that feminists do not hate men. And she says that those women on television who take their tops off, and scream and yell, are not feminists. They are radical revolutionists. Feminists, she tells me, only want the same respect and opportunities that men already take for granted.

Linda has also started using big words like "patriarchy" before she gives me a certain look. I decided that I'd better wake up and smell the coffee. Gone are the days when a man can speak freely. Her dad remembers his father saying in the presence of the women, that, "the country went to pot when women got the right to vote."

I scanned her course materials. Surprise! Surprise! Women write most of the stuff and some of those women are on the edge. And I began paying attention to her contacts, support groups and friends. That's when I found an e-mail from a female friend. Check this out.

A married couple goes on vacation to a fishing resort in northern Minnesota. The husband likes to fish at the crack of dawn. The wife likes to read. One morning the husband returns after several hours of fishing and decides to take a nap. Although not familiar with the lake, the wife decides to take the boat out. She motors out a short distance, anchors, and continues to read her book. Along comes a game warden in his boat. He pulls up alongside the woman and says, "Good morning Ma'am. What are you doing?" "I'm reading a book. (thinking "isn't that obvious?") "You're in a restricted fishing area," he informs her. "I'm sorry officer, but I'm not fishing. I'm reading." Yes, but you have all the equipment. I'll have to take you in and write you up." "If you do that, I'll have to charge you with sexual assault," says the woman. "But I haven't even touched you," says the man. "That's true, but you have all the equipment." MORAL: Never argue with a woman who reads. It's likely she can also think.

143

I SEE ANOTHER MORAL: Think twice before giving *"permission"* to your wife's further education and career pursuits.*

---

* *When this story was originally sent to the "True Tales" column the editor warned me that there would probably be repercussions. "I will be very surprised," he said, "if there are not 3 or 4 letters to the editor." I was relieved that there were no nasty letters but I did hear that I was a woman hater. And my wife was told that one does not even joke about these issues—see the last sentence—permission?*

I would like all readers to know that I do love at least one woman even if she claims to have her version of feminist leanings.

Chapter 52

The Feminist Solution

What came first, the chicken or the egg, the woman or the man? My feminist wife knows that Adam was created first and that Eve was fashioned from one of his ribs. In fact, it was Adam who gave Eve her name and the name "woman" is all tied up with the man.

I heard somewhere that God was going to create a super, fantastic woman but the cost was an arm and a leg. So Adam asked, "What could I get for a rib?" It's serious when a feminist stops laughing so I was most relieved when my wife shared this other anecdote with me:

In answer to the question, how do you decide whom to marry, a 10-year-old boy said, "You got to find somebody who likes the same stuff. Like, if you like sports, she should like it that you like sports, and she should keep the chips and dip coming."

God showed equality by using material from Adam's side. And when God made man, women were included in the very terminology. But the first marriage went tragically wrong. And the treatment of women, and women's rights, must be viewed from that standpoint.

It is important to remember that God wrote some unchanging laws on tables of stone and placed them *in the ark*. Some other laws were written by Moses and placed *in the side* of the ark.

Jesus said that some laws were given because of the hardness of men's hearts. And He went on to explain that a woman and a man were to be as "one." He also said that God's original plan was much different. The women loved him.

But the apostle Paul does say that wives are to submit to their husbands and that the husband is the head of the wife. I submit that whatever Paul had in mind would not be contentious if men would remember that Paul also said that men were to love their wives even as "...Christ loved the church and gave himself for it."

Once we thought we heard a burglar in the house. When I asked who should get out of bed to check things out, my feminist wife's response was immediate. "You're the man!" she said, and then she punched me.

The man who really treats his wife as he treats himself, and in fact, considers her needs and wishes before his own (Eph. 5: 28, 29) to the point of sacrifice, is a pretty good man indeed.

On occasion I've quoted just the part about the man being the head, before giving my happy-face grin. Now my wife has studied the whole chapter. But there's one passage that I'm saving.

Peter and Paul were leaders in the early Christian church and Paul says that he one time "confronted Peter to his face" over a certain issue. I find that encouraging. Anyway, these guys were contemporaries and buddies, so I find something that Peter said of Paul, to be very interesting. I'm keeping this last verse for sometime when my wife starts using all my best arguments against me.

If I should start losing ground I will quote to her how Peter said that Paul writes some things that are hard to understand and that "unlearned and unstable" people wrest his writings and also the other scriptures, unto their own destruction (2 Peter 3:16). On second thought, I wonder why she's never used that one on me.

Chapter 53

The Cross

In the Bible we find references to the mythological characters who surface repeatedly in the various pagan religions of the world. By combining the pieces, we get a story that tells of a powerful man named Nimrod. He founded the city of Babylon, which has always been antagonistic, and opposed, to God. After his death, his wife claimed to have experienced a miraculous pregnancy through the rays of the sun, representative of his continuing life and power. His primary symbols were sun and serpent, representing life without end.

The woman became known down through history as the *Queen of Heaven* and had various names in different cultures, probably as a result of God confusing the languages at the Tower of Babel (Gen. 11:9). One of her Babylonian names was Ishtar, from which we get our word, *Easter.* (According to the dictionary and Assyrian and Babylonian Mythology, Ishtar is the goddess of love and fertility, and also of war.)

The supposed virgin birth took place on December 25. The son, Tammuz, was the reincarnation of the father Nimrod, Lord of Heaven. The *true* Lord of heaven, let His people know through the prophet Ezekiel., how affronted He was with their seasonal services for Tammuz and the associated worship of the sun (Eze. 8:14-16). Mother and son were honored with cakes inscribed with a T. God was dishonored (Jer. 7:14-19). Even today, hot cross buns are a customary treat for the Easter season.

The cross is symbolic of Tammuz, the reincarnated Nimrod, and ultimately, Satan himself. Satan, sun and serpent all intertwine in a strange mix of deception. Jesus was crucified on a symbol of the Sun god; the Son of the true God was left in the clutches and darkness of the enemy.

146

Strangely, there is an Old Testament story of a serpent being elevated on a pole (Num. 21:8, 9). The people were directed to look to the serpent that they might live after poisonous snakes had bitten them. But the serpent represents darkness and lies and Satan himself. (John 8:44; Gen. 3:4; Rev. 12:9, 20:2). Why look to this infamous and deceptive symbol for life?

The answer lies in the nature of Jesus' death. He died a worst sinner's death-without hope, and God turned from Jesus and left him to suffer the penalty alone. He *became sin* for us (2 Cor. 5:21). Cursed is anyone hung on a tree (Deut. 21:23). Jesus redeemed us by taking on this curse (Gal. 3:13). He was numbered with the transgressors (Isa. 53:12; Luke 22:37).

But when our Lord suffered the death of the ultimate sinner, sin also died on the cross. How ironic that the symbol could be applied to Jesus, but really represented the death of Satan. It must have been with horror that Satan heard those words "It is finished" (John 19:30). "Father, into your hands, I commit my spirit" (Luke 23:46). When the body of Jesus went limp, there must have been a moment of awful recognition, before the earth literally shook and the rocks split (Matt. 27:51).

In the time of Esther, Haman made a gallows for Mordecai. But it was Haman himself who hung from those very gallows (Esther 7:10). That's not the way it was supposed to be. Similarly, in the sacrifice of Jesus, it was really Satan's death that was assured.

Jesus was supposed to crack. Satan risked more and more as he exerted increasing pressure. Death was release for Jesus, salvation for us, and an anti-climactic failure for Satan!

Terrible hate delights in pain and suffering, but final death brings only recognition of senseless destruction. So it must have been for Satan.

When Eve met Satan, she failed and began to die. When Satan met Jesus, *he* failed and began to die. And thus were fulfilled the words spoken anciently to the serpent, "I will put enmity between thee and the woman, and between thy seed and her seed; he shall bruise thy head, and thou shalt bruise his heel" (Gen. 3:15; Rev. 12:17).

The cross is a paradox. It represents both death and life, innocence, and yet everything evil. There is a bleeding lamb, the outstretched innocent and perfect Son of God who was also the son of man. There is an evil serpent wrapped around the emblem of Satan himself.

There are those who point to the cross in mockery. They see a dead and impotent failure, conquered by the ruler and prince of this world (2 Cor. 4:4; John 14:30, 16:11; Eph. 6:12). But there are many others who kneel in humble thankfulness at the foot of the cross recognizing the one who ... "ever lives to make intercession for them" (Heb. 7:25). How true! Jesus interceded for us by way of the awful crucifixion and it is this sacrifice, which allows Him to intercede for us still.

By His death, Jesus destroys him who holds the power of death—that is, the devil—and frees those who all their lives were held in slavery (Heb. 2:14, 15). "Therefore He is able to save completely those who come to God through Him, because He always lives to intercede for them" (Heb. 7:25).

When we speak of the cross, we really speak of the living Christ who now lives in us. We are to make known... "among the Gentiles the glorious riches of this mystery which is Christ in you, the hope of glory" (Col. 1:27). The cross itself has no merit. It is not a piece of jewellery to be worn around one's neck. Neither is it something to be venerated. Anciently, the bronze serpent, Nehushtan, so full of meaning and hope for the people of Israel, had to be destroyed, when they began actually to worship it (2 Kings 18:4).

Can you imagine the horror? All too often, our confusion and ignorance has allowed Satan to laugh loudly in the face of our Creator and Redeemer. Several verses previous to this one, is this sad commentary: "Even while these people were worshipping the Lord, they were serving their idols" (2 Kings 17:41).

All the mythologies of the world come face to face with the truth of the one and only saving gospel of Jesus Christ, when we view the cross correctly. "Salvation is found in no one else, for there is no other name under heaven given to men by which we must be saved" (Acts 4:12).

Paul, the great defender of the cross, has said, "For the message of the cross is foolishness to those who are perishing, but to us who are being saved it is the power of God" (1 Cor. 1:18). "I resolved to know nothing while I was with you except Jesus Christ and him crucified (1 Cor. 2:2). "None of the rulers of this age understood it, for if they had, they would not have crucified the Lord of glory" (1 Cor. 2:8). "I have been crucified with Christ and I no longer live, but Christ lives in me. The life I live in the body, I live by faith in the Son of God, who loved me" (Gal. 2:20). "Christ redeemed us from the curse of the law by becoming a curse for us, for it is written: 'Cursed is everyone who is hung on a tree'" (Gal. 3:13). "May I never boast except in the cross of our Lord Jesus Christ, through which the world has been crucified to me, and I to the world" (Gal. 6:14).

Have you learned to boast in the cross of Jesus Christ our Lord? Has your sinful self been crucified with Him? Are you marked with His marks of ownership? Listen to Paul's final words to the Galatians and to us: "Finally, let no one cause me trouble, for I bear on my body the marks of Jesus. The grace of our Lord Jesus Christ be with your spirit, brothers. Amen" (Gal. 6:17, 18).

For many, the Easter fertility celebration (bunnies, eggs etc.) is just a time for mythological fun and frivolity. Others remember the one who claimed to be the resurrected Saviour of the world. He promises the ultimate destruction of the serpent, also depicted in the story of the cross. Thus, two ancient streams of thought clash together in one amazing up-lifted symbol.

The first book of the Bible has the *city* of Babylon and the term is associated with "confusion." The languages were confounded, or confused, at the *tower* of Babel, or Babylon, and the people scattered. The *nation* of Babylon sought to change Israel's religion and incorporate the people into their system. The last book of the Bible has a dire warning against the *church* of Babylon (Gen. 10:10, 11:9; Isa. 14:4-19; Daniel; and Rev. 17:5, 18:1-24).

Serpent and flying dragon—Nepal

Sisutl - the double headed, flying serpent and
dragon — Port Hardy, B.C

Frog - transformer coming from the mouth of
the dragon and riding a canoe

150

Fire breathing flying dragon — Nepal

Caddo Indian winged serpent Uktena and solar cross.
Caddos lived in the southeast United States.
(Released under the GNU Free Documentation Liscense)

151

Partial views of floating houses

Mr. Blue

The silent killer

Author feeding Otskar   Not a Pet

Lingcod like the
one Otskar killed

Gary McGill with the wolf eel
Otskar ate live from the tail

Speckie - A story for
another time

A good day

Otskar - photo courtesy
of Ken Knopp

Fur seal warming by the stove

Chapter 54

The Great Tree of Babylon

Alexander Hislop explains the ancient pagan custom of the Christmas "yule log." The log burned in the fire and then a new sprout or "rebirth" was symbolized in the Christmas tree. The divine child or god, conceived at Easter and born on Christmas day, was known as Baal-berith, "Lord of the Covenant." With the change of one letter, he was also known as Baal-bereth, "Lord of the fir tree." In his book, The Two Babylons, Hislop says, "Now the Yule Log is the dead stock of Nimrod, deified as the sun-god, but cut down by his enemies; the slain god come to life again" (Alexander Hislop, *The Two Babylons*, p. 97, 98).

Hislop says further, "Now the great god, cut off in the midst of his power and glory, was symbolized as a huge tree, stripped of all its branches, and cut down almost to the ground. But the great serpent, the symbol of the life restoring Aesculapius, twists itself around the dead stock and lo, at its side up sprouts a young tree—a tree of an entirely different kind, that is destined never to be cut down by hostile power—even the palm-tree, the well-known symbol of victory. The Christmas-tree, as has been stated, was generally at Rome a different tree, even the fir"... (Ibid., p. 98).

This story is especially pertinent when one considers something God said of Lucifer. "How art thou fallen from heaven, O Lucifer, son of the morning! How art thou cut down to the ground; which didst weaken the nations! For thou hast said in thine heart, I will ascend into heaven, I will exalt my throne above the stars of God; I will sit also upon the mount of the congregation, in the sides of the north: I will ascend above the heights of the clouds; I will be like the most High" (Isa. 14:12-14).

When God spoke to the king of Tyre, He suddenly began addressing the unseen power behind the nation. Fire would not bring forth any kind of new birth, but would instead, destroy this mighty angel and burn him to ashes and he would be no more (Eze. 28).

It is fascinating to realize that God was speaking to the king of Babylon in a similar fashion, when He spoke of Lucifer as being "cut to the ground." And he also said that the king would be cast out of his grave like an "abominable branch" (Isa. 14:12, 19).

Similar symbolism is seen again when King Nebuchadnezzar dreams of a great tree that is cut down to the stump. This stump is wrapped, not with a serpent, but with a band of iron and brass, for seven years. And the human king mimics his satanic master when he says, "Is not this great Babylon that I have built for the house of the kingdom by the might of my power, and for the honour of my majesty?" (Dan. 4).

Long before, God had said to His people, "If ye will not yet for all this hearken unto me, then I will punish you seven times more for your sins. And I will break the pride of your power; and I will make your heaven as iron, and your earth as brass." (Lev. 26:18, 19). Thus, it would appear that God's name is written all over Nebuchadnezzar's story.

God uses brass and iron to represent discipline, strength and protection, and this is sometimes done simultaneously (Lev. 26:18, 19; Jer. 1:18, 19, 15:20; Deut. 33:25; Dan. 4). And the word "band" is used in a restrictive sense as well. This word in the Hebrew corresponds to manacles, bonds, or some similar form of imprisonment (*Strong's Concordance*).

Lucifer was cut down (not destroyed) and has never repented. In the form of a serpent, he deceived Eve at a specific *tree*—the tree of knowledge of good and evil. He claims to resurrect himself from God's edict and offers his worthless promises to us. He makes it appear that the dead are not really dead, and with ceremonies like "firewalking" he would have us believe that the future hell-fire is of no concern either.

Babylon's false teachings as symbolized by the serpent and its mystic number 666 have spread around the world. But in the very heart of ancient Babylon, God cut the kingly tree down and bound the stump with a band of iron and brass, signifying both strength and protection. And king Nebuchadnezzar was plucked like a brand or "branch from the burning." After 7 years (God's number) Nebuchadnezzar, unlike his spiritual mentor, did repent, and he acknowledged the God of heaven and earth.

Satan was cut down to the ground and mythology shows his stump entwined by a serpent. The Bible represented him as the power behind the nations of Tyre and Babylon (Eze. 28; Isa. 14). Nebuchadnezzar, depicted as a mighty tree, was also cut down but the stump was bound with a band of iron and brass (Dan. 4). And the real branch that sprang forth from the root of David and Jessie, humbled, and then liberated this king. What an amazing twist and play on words!

Christ is the only tree or living branch that springs forth to offer life—real, eternal life. "Behold the days come, saith the LORD, that I will raise unto David a righteous Branch, and a King shall reign and prosper, and shall execute judgment and justice in the earth." "I Jesus have sent mine angel to testify unto you these things in the churches. I am the root and the offspring of David, and the bright and morning star." He says to us, "...Fear not; I am the first and the last: I am he that liveth, and was dead; and, behold, I am alive for evermore, Amen; and have the keys of hell and of death" (Jer. 23:5, 33:15; Isa. 11:1; Zech. 3:8, 6:12; Rev. 1:17, 18, 22:16).

Joseph Campbell says in his book, *The Power of Myth*: "I think it's Cicero who says that when you go into a great tall grove, the presence of a deity becomes known to you. There are sacred groves everywhere. Going into the forest as a little boy, I can remember worshipping a tree, a great big old tree, thinking, 'My, my, what you've known and been.' I think this sense of the presence of creation is a basic mood of man" (p. 92).

Look up the word "groves" in *Strong's Concordance*. There is a connection to the Canaanite Asherah. Even in the dictionary Asherah is defined thus: "a tree or pole found beside the altar in a Canaanite high place and held to be sacred to the goddess Asherah" (Jer. 2:20, 17:2).

Chapter 55

One More Christmas

I remember my little daughter repeating to a friend, a yuletide phrase her Grandpa often used, "Santa is a fake." A nearby man exclaimed to me, "Can you believe it? The kids don't even believe in Santa Claus anymore."

Grandpa (on my wife's side) told us every year that he hated Christmas. It wasn't really true, but he often got himself in trouble with Grandma for waiting too long. And then he rushed to find a tree that would fill the designated corner. He did the same with gift shopping; it seems he waited till the last minute and did not put enough thought into this seasonal act of love. So to make up for his obvious neglect, he would go shopping again for something really grand this time. When Grandma smiled again, that signaled the beginning of peace and good tidings of joy.

In recent years, some politicians have banned certain traditional music and displays that might be deemed "religious." Christmas is recognized for its Christian themes as presented in the story of Jesus' birth. I guess that's why one school district superintendent decided that Christmas should be completely banished from her schools. (B.C. parliament buildings, Nanaimo school district superintendent, 2002.)

Many would be surprised to find that some people within all denominations avoid Christmas because of its "pagan" roots. And one church—the Jehovah's Witnesses—with a membership in the millions, seeks to avoid Christmas entirely.

That is difficult because we are steeped in various forms of religious observance from antiquity. Sometimes these things are much more important than we realize, but in other cases, the significance of our traditions has long been forgotten. And most do not really believe in a virgin birth. The stories of Jesus are blended into the other world mythologies. His name means "Savior" but He is mostly ignored.

One More Christmas

The Catholic Saint Nicholas was imported to North America by way of the Dutch. But English settlers, wanting nothing Catholic, resurrected the older Germanic version. Behind the name Santa Claus actually stands the figure of the pagan god Thor, after whom Thursday is named (Francis X. Weiser, *Handbook of Christian Feasts and Customs,* p. 89).

Thor was represented as an elderly, jovial, heavy man with a long white beard, who lived in the North. His element was the fire, his color red. Two white goats named Cracker and Gnasher drew his chariot and the rumble and roar of thunder were said to be caused by the rolling of the chariot's wheels. The fireplace was sacred to him and he was said to come down the chimney into his element, the fire (Ibid., p.90, 91).

The first Jesuit missionaries to Tibet, China and Japan were astonished to find the counterpart of the Madonna and her child. The virgin birth story was also taught in South America. As mythologist Joseph Campbell says, "...the early Christian missionaries were forced to think that the devil himself must be throwing up mockeries of their teaching..." (Alexander Hislop, *The Two Babylons,* p. 20, 21; and Joseph Campbell, *The Hero With a Thousand Faces,* p. 309). And indeed, something interesting happens when one simply juggles Santa's letters around.

The original stories can be traced back to the ancient Babylon of Nimrod. Nimrod is known in various cultures as Baal, Ninus, Zeus, Jupiter, Ra, and Odin. His wife Semiramis was also Ashtoreth, Astarte, Cybele, Diana, Frigg, Freyia, and Ishtar—our "Easter." (William Josiah Sutton, *The Antichrist 666.* A good dictionary or encyclopedia will often show the same relationships in names and origins. In addition, the book *The Two Babylons* traces the history.)

Nimrod died and became known as the sun god. He impregnated his wife by way of the sun's rays, and the virgin birth took place nine months later (Easter to Christmas) on December 25. The stock of Nimrod was represented as a Yule log or stump, entwined by the serpent, Aesculapius. The pagan god-child, Tammuz, was also known as Baal-bereth, "Lord of the Fir-Tree" (*The Two Babylons,* p. 98; and *The Antichrist 666,* p. 30. Both books contain numerous references to other works).

Some of the parallel names for Tammuz were Bacchus, Hercules, Dionysus, Attis, Krishna, Quetzalcoatl and Balder. He was variously known as both the husband and the son of the mother because he was reincarnated. And his birth coincided with the "sun" seeming to come to life as the days began to lengthen after the winter solstice (*The Two Babylons,* p. 22; *The Antichrist 666,* p. 42).

The Aztec Quetzalcoatl was born of a virgin and the "*morning star*" Venus was his symbol. The name means "feathered serpent" and he was depicted as the serpent god and had a white human type form as well. It was believed that he would return some day (*The Antichrist 666,* p. 94-96. Numerous internet sources on mythology).

Alexander Hislop points out that "Yule" is the Chaldee name for an infant or little child, and the 25th of December was called by our pagan Anglo-Saxon ancestors, "Yule-day. And he also says, "Now the Yule Log is the dead stock of Nimrod, deified as the sun-god, but cut down by his enemies; the Christmas-tree is Nimrod redivivus—the slain god come to life again" (*The Two Babylons,* p. 93, 98).

It is important to see the similarities between Jesus and Santa and also the differences. Just like Jesus, Santa sees and knows everything, whether we're naughty or nice, as the song says. And both bring gifts. Both are depicted as caring deeply for us and something about the "north" is common to both.

See if these Bible verses do not have a ring of familiarity. "How art thou fallen from heaven, O Lucifer, son of the morning! How art thou cut down to the ground; which didst weaken the nations! For thou hast said in thine heart, I will ascend into heaven, I will exalt my throne above the stars of God; I will sit also upon the mount of the congregation, in the sides of the north: I will ascend above the heights of the clouds; I will be like the most High" (Isa. 14:12-14).

"Thou art the anointed cherub that covereth; and I have set thee so: thou wast upon the holy mountain of God; thou hast walked up and down in the midst of the stones of fire" (Eze. 28:14).

"I beheld till the thrones were cast down, and the Ancient of days did sit, whose garment was white as snow, and the hair of his head like the pure wool: his throne was like the fiery flame, and his wheels as burning fire" (Dan. 7:9).

"His head and his hairs were white like wool, as white as snow; and his eyes were as a flame of fire; And his feet like unto fine brass, as if they burned in a furnace; and his voice as the sound of many waters" (Rev. 1:14, 15).

"And there shall come forth a rod out of the stem of Jesse, and a Branch shall grow out of his roots" (Isa. 11:1).

"Behold the days come, saith the LORD, that I will raise unto David a righteous Branch, and a King shall reign and prosper, and shall execute judgment and justice in the earth" (Jer. 23:5).

"And behold, I come quickly; and my reward is with me, to give every man according as his work shall be" (Rev. 22:12).

"I Jesus have sent mine angel to testify unto you these things in the churches. I am the root and the offspring of David, and the bright and morning star" (Rev. 22:16).

The serpent deceived Adam and Eve in the beginning (Gen. 3). Jesus said that Satan was a liar from the beginning (John 8). He wanted to be worshipped like God (Isa. 14). He is a pretender, an evil trickster (2 Cor. 11:14). The Bible identifies him as the serpent and dragon (Rev. 12:7, 9).

Satan was cut down to the ground and mythology shows his stump entwined by a serpent. The Bible represented him as the power behind the nations of Tyre and Babylon (Eze. 28; Isa. 14). Nebuchadnezzar, depicted as a mighty tree, was also cut down but the stump was bound with a band of iron and brass (Dan. 4). And the real branch that sprang forth from the root of David and Jessie, humbled, and then liberated this king. What an amazing twist and play on words!

The symbol for Tammuz was a cross, a T. He was supposed to have conquered death and offered life. Satan himself, is the mastermind behind all these systems; and they are referred to as the "mystery religions"

Amazingly, Jesus died on a cross and came to life again, promising us the possibility of the same. He died in the Spring—a time of renewal and life. So, in effect, He took the devil's symbol and made it real in the sacrifice of himself for the human race. It seems that all paths do not lead to the same end. There is only one path that leads to eternal life, and it is so radically different, that one can only wonder how and why Satan has been so wildly successful as he continues to dupe us.

The Bible story gives the world the "gift" of Jesus. His favorite title was "Son of Man." And nearly two thousand years ago, he asked, "When the Son of man comes again, will he find faith on the earth?"

Chapter 56

Products of Time

We are products of time beginning with our birth. Our waking, working and sleeping are regulated by time and time dictates when we play and when we worship. The concept of seventh-day worship time has an ancient history among languages, peoples and cultures.

The day, month and year come from astronomical earth-moon-sun relationships. But the 7-day weekly cycle comes from someplace else. Of all the world's festivals the weekly Sabbath is the oldest.

The Biblical days of creation began with the evening. In the same manner Israel was commanded to observe Sabbath from evening to evening (Lev. 23:32). This is a practice the Jews carry on to this day. We inherited from the Romans, our day that begins and ends with midnight, but even the more recent observance of *Sunday* as a Christian day of worship was once recognized to extend from sundown Saturday to sundown Sunday.

In our culture the night before New Year's Day is still known as New Year's Eve and the night before Christmas as Christmas Eve. And there's Halloween (hallowed evening). These terms are remnants of the European custom of beginning the day with sunset.

Products of Time

The day and thus the Sabbath come to us as the earth spins. When Magellan's men first circumnavigated the globe they were puzzled to find their time calculations one day off. They had not taken into account that as they followed the sun they eventually gained a day.

We assume that the ancients knew nothing of this problem or even that the earth was round. But long before the time of Magellan or Columbus the Bible had recorded, "God sits above the circle of the earth and its inhabitants are like grasshoppers" (Isa. 40:22). "He hangs the earth on nothing" (Job 26:7).

Amazingly, in over 100 languages of the world, the seventh day, Saturday, is called the Sabbath. This word (Rest Day) has an ancient history. *Some* people, *somewhere* on earth, have always observed this Sabbath.

It may come as a surprise to learn that even today millions of people cease regular work at sundown Friday evening to begin a special day of honor and recognition to the Creator of heaven and earth.

The two largest groups still holding to this practice are the Jews, of course, and Seventh-day Adventists. As a Seventh-day Adventist myself, I once wrote a short letter to the editor of a commercial fishing magazine explaining very briefly why the Sabbath could not be a regular work day for us. His response was pointed. "It's about time!" he said (no pun intended). Here is a portion of the article.

(1) We believe our world's seven-day weekly cycle comes directly from Creation week (Gen. 2:2, 3).

(2) The seventh day, called Sabbath (Rest day), was set aside as a memorial to the Creator. The 4th commandment reads, "Remember the Sabbath day, to keep it holy. Six days shalt thou labour, and do all thy work: But the seventh day is the Sabbath of the LORD thy God: in it thou shalt not do any work, thou, nor thy son, nor thy daughter thy manservant, nor thy maidservant, nor thy cattle, nor thy stranger that is within thy gates: For in six days the LORD made heaven and earth, the sea, and all that in them is, and rested the seventh day: wherefore the LORD blessed the Sabbath day, and hallowed it" (Ex. 20:8-11).

163

(3) In many languages, the word for Sabbath is synonymous with Saturday, for example, Russian-Subbota, Italian-Sabbato. This makes sense because Jesus said the Sabbath was made for mankind and that He was "Lord of the Sabbath" (Mark 2:27, 28).

(4) Jesus observed the Bible Sabbath (Luke 4:16) and expected Christians to do likewise (Matt. 24:20).

(5) The seventh day is Saturday as most calendars will show. The Jews have been keeping track of the weekly cycle for thousands of years.

(6) The Sabbath is a joyful celebration. The Bible says, "If you love me, keep my commandments" (John 14:15). Jesus is at the heart of our religion, -not the Sabbath, but He is the reason for its existence.

Interesting, this idea of Sabbath rest time. *Sabbath* is a memorial of creation. As Jewish, Seventh-day Adventist author Clifford Goldstein explains, "In a manner so powerful that, without the possibility of exception, it consumes 24 hours a week of our lives, the Sabbath confronts us with the realization that our life, breath, and existence come only from the Creator."

Whether one accepts this concept as a product of myth, custom, or fact, it is nonetheless true that *time* connects us to our earth and to each other. Is it actually possible that there is an element of time designed to connect us to our creator?

A five-part documentary titled "The Seventh Day—Revelations from the Lost Pages of History" has been produced on this subject. It is hosted by Hal Holbrook.

Chapter 57

Wolves Don't Bite

After attacking a sleeping kayaker in July of 2000, two wolves were shot near Tofino, on Vancouver Island's west coast. Actual predatory attacks are rare but they do occur.

I think perhaps we should treat wolves with the same cautious respect that my little dog shows them. To him, fresh tracks are very, very interesting indeed and his hackles rise with a stiff sense of caution and possible danger. The smell of cougar, on the other hand, produces growling and barking on the order of panic and pandemonium.

I sometimes wonder what *documented* means. Must someone be bitten and torn, or must a biologist with letters behind his name be present to verify? An Australian woman spent seven years in prison accused of murdering her own child, because people could not believe that a dingo (a wild wolf-like dog) would attack a human. Coyotes are becoming a real problem in the Fraser valley and a child was harassed and nipped by one recently.

I remember an interesting experience my wife and I had several years back. One evening we were cruising Smith Inlet with a little boat, when a deer came crashing out of the woods and into the water. It swam frantically across the inlet, which was a fair distance. I shut the outboard off and soon a big wolf loped out of the woods but turned back immediately as soon as it saw us. Wolves have been known to stay on the track of deer, even if it means swimming after them. We sometimes found deer drowned in the log boom, after having been trapped there by wolves.

Ernie Knopp once rescued a buck from the water and brought it to camp to regain its strength. It was so tired, it could not even stand. Later, I saw a wolf staring at camp from the shore, probably less than 100 feet away. Ernie got his .303 rifle, aimed while everyone watched expectantly, and blasted away. I wondered how on earth he could have missed, and then I heard my parents say that he had not wanted to kill the wolf in front of all the children.

165

My dad had sort of a hair-raising encounter with a pack of wolves. This was an experience he had no desire to repeat, no matter what documented statistics might show. This is his story...

"Many years ago, I traveled by speedboat to Smith Inlet to check on our logging camp and equipment. It was the beginning of winter, logging had ceased and the camp had been temporarily vacated. Some of the heavy equipment needed to be winterized and as it turned out, I had to hike about three miles up a road through timber. I started a little too late in the day and hadn't calculated that the snow would be deeper further along.

About three-quarters of the way to my destination, I approached a bridge, and on the other side was a pack of wolves. They showed no fear and in fact the biggest one advanced aggressively, growling and showing its teeth. I was too far along to turn back and was afraid to retreat, as this may have made the wolves even bolder. The snow hampered me somewhat and nightfall was not far distant.

I picked up two sticks and banged them together and walked towards the wolves screaming and yelling in a bluff. I would have been pleased if the effect had been more telling, but the big wolf did at least back up a few feet and step off the road, as did the others. Unfortunately they fell in behind me and followed me all the way to my destination.

It was cold and my D-7 Cat would not start. As the evening shadows developed, the wolves began to howl. In the winter when the woods are deathly silent and one is all alone, the silence itself can be unnerving, but the howling of wolves certainly does not help one's anxiety!

I built a fire under the cat to warm the engine and hoped desperately that I would not have to spend the night on guard. To my great relief, my machine did start with a welcome roar and I was able to return to camp. I would never again walk alone in these woods without a rifle.

I've heard that wolves don't attack people but I know of two forestry officers who spent the better part of a day up in a tree. Like these officers, I was not convinced enough to test this assumption. In my case, I am certainly glad I did not climb a tree or I may have been found frozen in the branches, or is it possible that my bones could have been scattered at its base?"

Chapter 58

Little Tyke

A peacock was dancing and turning to show the absolutely fantastic colors and designs to be found in his fanned tail. I heard someone remark about the intricate patterns and I said that it was the peacock's tail feathers and the human eye that had given Charles Darwin the shudders.

The Bible says that "…since the creation of the world God's invisible qualities—his eternal power and divine nature - have been clearly seen, being understood from what has been made, so that men are without excuse." But there is another message that is puzzling.

I once had a gentle, little kitten that had been separated from its mother at an early age and had not had opportunity to be trained in the way of cats. One day I trapped a mouse and I decided to see what this kitten's reaction would be when it saw a mouse for the first time ever.

I tied a string to the tail of the mouse and dragged it across the floor. To my surprise, the kitten attacked the mouse with extended claws and tried to run away with it. It was deadly serious and wanted nothing to do with me. In fact, it was guarding the mouse zealously and refused to share it. But that's what cats do, right?

And then there is my daughter's cat—"Black Jasper." He loves to hunt birds and he too, had no teacher. He is mesmerized by the television if a bird should flit across the screen. My wife says that he is the picture of evil. She may be right; his eyes go squinty and he makes a strange sound of frustration and rage. But isn't that the way cats are and the way cats have always been? Maybe not.

"Little Tyke" is the amazing, true story of a world-famous, vegetarian, African lion. The book was published in 1956 and written by Georges H. Westbeau. This lion was raised from a tiny kitten and it refused to eat meat. It loved people and every kind of animal and was always gentle. It was featured on film, and the media loved it.

This vegetarian lion reacted with fear, to meat, maybe because it smelled fear and terror in the flesh of the animals that had been slaughtered. The first time the lion was offered a bone; it threw up. Because scientists said the lion could not live without meat, its owners were quite concerned.

At four years of age and 350 pounds, the lion still refused meat, so the owners offered a thousand dollar reward to anyone who could come up with an enticing formula. Amazingly, the lion would not drink milk with even one drop of blood in it.

One day a young visitor wondered why they were worried. He asked, "Don't you read your Bible?" He directed them to the very first chapter. "And to every beast of the earth, and to every fowl of the air, and to everything that creepeth upon the earth, wherein there is life, I have given every green herb for meat: and it was so."

The Bible promises a restoration, soon, to what was originally intended. In the meantime, we are part of an awful experiment that our first parents started. Mostly, we are infected through heredity just like "Black Jasper."

As we look around, we see the results of evil. But was the whole world once in perfect harmony? And do we once in awhile get a glimpse of what used to be? The Bible records the story of Jesus talking to a man named Nicodemus. Jesus told him that we must be born again and that it was similar to the wind which cannot be seen but produces indisputable results. Have you ever met someone who has been re-born?

Chapter 59

The New Woman

My kids were looking all over the church for the new woman but couldn't spot her even though some friends were carefully pointing to where she was sitting. My children were looking for someone who stood out from the crowd but they didn't realize that the new woman was sitting in the pew directly in front of them.

To me, she appeared to be a well-dressed and pleasant looking middle-aged lady. But my wife said that her hands were too big. The new woman was causing quite a kerfluffle in her conservative, Bible believing congregation because she had previously been a prominent church leader and the father of two children.

This may sound confusing because it is; the man had put his church in quite a pickle. In midlife he had decided on a sex change operation but was he really now a woman? Had God simply made a mistake as he put it? Which bathroom did he/she now use? The women did not want her in theirs so the pastor said that she could use his private office facilities.

To some, this was all very serious. To others it was disturbing, to say the least, but to many there was something sort of humorous about the whole affair. And then there was the problem of the guide book. When we mold the Bible to suit our wants—it becomes *our* book, not *His*.

Since the Bible is unchanging in its condemnation of same sex relations in both the Old Testament and the New Testament (see Lev. 18:13, 22; 20:13; Rom. 1:26, 27; 1 Cor. 1:26, 27), we need a solution. Some people categorize homosexual sin as especially offensive to God. But homosexual sin is just one sin among many that is called an abomination.

Homosexuals often claim to have been born homosexual but the important thing to remember, is that when we are sinking in sin—it will do us in—we need a Savior. A former homosexual explains that for a drowning victim, it matters not whether he fell into the water, was pushed in, or jumped in. When a person is drowning, he needs a lifeguard and when he accepts that fact, the lifeguard can help. Jesus is that lifeguard.

In the clergy column of my town's local paper, a pastor took the view that the Bible's death penalty for serving other gods and teaching the same, was no longer applicable. And the idea was developed that if we cannot take this literally, then it is time to also revisit the gay and lesbian issue and the relationship to church. The clergy article closed by saying that even Jesus himself would be fully supportive of the blessing of same sex couples. Really?

It is true that some Old Testament laws were given "for the hardness of men's hearts" (Matt. 19:8). An "eye for an eye and a tooth for a tooth" might be an example of an exacting justice for people who had only known the cruel and unjust rule of slavery, but Jesus expanded and explained the principles involved (Matt. 5:17-47). His instruction concerning forgiveness and divorce is still radical today.

The Bible called the people of Israel, as they came from Egyptian slavery, a mixed multitude and a rebellious people. But these people entered into a covenant with God whose voice they actually heard and whose miracles they witnessed. We call their form of government, a theocracy, because they were under the direct leadership of God himself. As evidence, they could travel by day or by night because of a miraculous pillar of cloud and pillar of fire (Ex. 13:21, 22).

We operate under a democratic form of government today, and not a theocracy. When Jesus walked the earth, the people were ruled by Roman law and had broken their sacred covenant with God. The leaders tried to catch Jesus in a cruel trick when they brought a woman to him who had been caught in the very act of adultery. They asked him what should be done. If he upheld Old Testament punishment by death, they would accuse him to the authorities; but if he let the woman go, they would accuse him of ignoring their law.

There had always been a process before a death penalty could be carried out; for example, there had to be witnesses. To the surprise of the accusers, Jesus began writing on the ground and all the accusers left, beginning with the oldest. It appears that he exposed their

170

sins just as they had exposed the woman's sin. Then Jesus said to the woman, "Go and sin no more" (John 8:12). It is important to note that Jesus still called sin by its correct name and expected his followers to do the same.

The term "sodomy" comes from the story of a city that was destroyed by God for its sinfulness (Gen. 19). The principle that same sex relations are wrong is continued in the New Testament teachings. "Because of this, God gave them over to shameful lusts. Even their women exchanged natural relations for unnatural ones. In the same way the men also abandoned natural relations with women and were inflamed with lust for one another. Men committed indecent acts with other men, and received in themselves the due penalty for their perversion" (Rom. 1:26, 27, NIV). "...Do not be deceived: Neither the sexually immoral nor idolaters nor adulterers nor male prostitutes nor homosexual offenders nor thieves nor the greedy nor drunkards nor slanderers nor swindlers will inherit the kingdom of God" (1 Cor. 6:9, 10, NIV).

Too often, this passage is quoted and ended without noting that there are sins mentioned other than sexual sins. But the next verse puts everything in perspective and upholds the good news of the gospel. It continues, "And that is what some of you were. But you were washed, you were sanctified, you were justified in the name of the Lord Jesus Christ and by the Spirit of our God" (verse 11).

Jesus showed us how to love those who believe differently without ignoring the sin. He still invites people to come to him just as they are, but he does not leave them the way they came. He is fully able to do for any of us just as He did for those people of the Corinthian church. "If we confess our sins, he is faithful and just to forgive us our sins, and to cleanse us from all unrighteousness" (1 John 1:9).

Ron Woolsey is an author and pastor who "came out" twice— once as a gay man and the second time as a straight, married pastor. Under his pen name, Victor J. Adamson, he wrote an excellent book That Kind Can Never Change! Can They...? *His Web site is www. victorjadamson.com.*

Chapter 60

Tongue Twisters

Sometimes we like tongue twisters and sometimes we don't. Sometimes we trick our tongues, but at other times, these powerful little instruments take on a life of their own and have fun at our expense. They can tie us up and cause us great mental anguish.

As kids we tried to repeat as fast as possible, "If Peter Piper picked a peck of pickled peppers, how many pickled peppers did Peter Piper pick?" And of course there was this old favorite, "How much wood could a woodchuck chuck if a woodchuck could chuck wood?"

Someone modified that old line with this: "How much wood could Chuck Woods' woodchuck chuck, if Chuck Woods' woodchuck could and would chuck wood? If Chuck Woods' woodchuck could and would chuck wood, how much wood could and would Chuck Woods' woodchuck chuck? Chuck Woods' woodchuck would chuck, he would, as much as he could, and chuck as much wood as any woodchuck would, if a woodchuck could and would chuck wood."

Another person said of twisters, "Mr. Tongue Twister tried to train his tongue to twist and turn, and twit and twat, to learn the letter ""T"."

I knew we were bored, many years ago, when the bunkhouse talk turned from jokes to tongue twisters. One of the boys invented this concoction: "If a bitter, biting bittern bit a bigger, bitter, biting bittern, would the bitten, bigger, bitter, biting bittern bite the bitter, biting bittern back?" (Tex Lyon or Lawrence Woodall will tell you that bitterns are very shy, wading birds, something like blue herons)

Let me give you just one more that's so difficult, it's disgusting, and more so because it takes some thought. It comes from a web site called, "International Collection of Tongue Twisters." Here goes: "Ed Nott was shot and Sam Shott was not. So it is better to be Shott than Nott. Some say Nott was not shot. But Shott says he shot Nott. Either the shot Shott shot at Nott was not shot, or Nott was shot. If the shot Shott shot shot Nott, Nott was shot. But if the shot Shott shot shot

Shott, the shot was Shott, not Nott. However, the shot Shott shot shot not Shott - but Nott. So, Ed Nott was shot and that's hot! Is it not?"

I remember a history teacher who told my class about a poor man who tried to introduce Herbert Hoover, president of the United States. He apparently said something like this: "Ladies and gentlemen, Hubert Herver, I mean, Herbert Herver, (pause) Hoobert," and then he completely gave up. "Anyway," he said, "He's going to talk to us."

I once had a man laying some linoleum on the galley floor of my boat. My little boy was with me, and I put a life belt on him and sent him to fish off the dock, but he became bored. He came back and was staring at the cigarette hanging from the carpet layer's mouth.

Because I knew that my little boy was just about to come out with some really embarrassing observation about the smoking, which wasn't hurting a thing, I decided to quickly ask him why he had given up on his fishing. That would change his focus. But to my horror, I heard my tongue say to my little 4-year old, "Kevin, have you given up on your smoking?" I quickly changed the last word.

The carpet layer winced. I could think of nothing further to say, and when you have nothing to say, you say nothing, so that is exactly what I did.

Chapter 61

Too Close for Comfort

My wife and I took the neatest trip at the end of May. We turned left after departing the Horseshoe Bay ferry terminal and drove through the Whistler mountains and on to Pemberton. The local hotel had character and the price was right.

We drove around the countryside the next morning and decided to check the hot springs out another time. Then we drove through fantastic scenery, with very little traffic, and on to Lillooet, and Cariboo country. Along the way we saw mountain goats, bighorn sheep, marmots and little pikas.

The William's Lake nature reserve was having a special weekend and we were introduced to a great-horned owl that had been imprinted. Birds are programmed to latch onto the first object they see and hear - which is supposed to be a parent. But when this owl had hatched, it had come in contact with a human and was forever ruined. It didn't know it was an owl.

We saw nesting loons and grebes and viewed pelicans and sandhill cranes. The singing of a multitude of birds was music to our ears as we hiked to the Fraser River. We learned that some of the pink salmon that pass Vancouver Island spawn in little tributary streams way up there. Then we traveled out to the Horsefly area where I had once lived. And horseflies attacked and bit us.

My wife suggested that we take an alternate route to Barkerville, but we did not realize that the road turned to gravel and wound through mountainous terrain. She became quiet and her body language was not reassuring as we traveled for hours. Then she tried to blame me for becoming stuck in the snow.

I had been telling her it was too hard to turn back but things kept deteriorating until I finally had to admit that we were in trouble. I wasn't sure that we "could" go back because it meant that our Ford Taurus wagon would have to take us uphill in places. We did have chains but I was not very confident. And during the whole trip we saw no other people.

It appeared that only one four-wheel-drive truck had gone through before us and it left us high centered but I dared not leave the track. I stopped the car and hiked ahead until I came to a place where approaching vehicles had stopped to return the other way—the direction we wished to go.

We had one chance. I gunned the engine and we slipped and slid our way along. My wife sat stiffly beside me. She was not impressed that we were the first car of the season to make it safely over the mountain pass. And the dozen or so bears that we had seen had not impressed her either (she saw those at home). A moose sighting hadn't helped and neither had a fantastic alpine lake that we would not have seen except for our adventure.

I knew things were serious so I drove as quickly as possible to the nearest hotel, in the community of Wells, near Barkerville. At $57 it was one of the best investments I ever made because my wife's attitude improved immensely. I have not yet been able to convince her that we should try the same route again. But I think if I give her more time, anything is possible.

Our trip continued through Quesnel, Prince George, Jasper and Banff - in the Canadian Rockies. We saw a grizzly and moose and elk. And we saw some strange things.

High in the mountains, we saw fossils of ancient marine life. And we even viewed a fossilized wave. The ripple marks recorded in the rock were just like the wave marks left in the sand of any ocean beach.

We spent our next night, in Radium, after a dip in the hot springs pool. Then we proceeded on to Idaho where my wife's parents live on 500 acres.

My wife enjoyed walking with the dog and he chased a moose twice, a bear, and several deer, grouse and turkeys. Her mother said that she should take a whistle for safety purposes. Linda did as her mother suggested—just to make her happy.

The last morning of our visit she went walking with the dog again and this time he got a mother elk riled up. The elk was furiously chasing the dog and trying to stomp him with her hooves. Linda jumped behind a tree and could have touched the elk as it went racing by.

The dog appeared to be looking for her and circled around to return, with the elk in hot pursuit. She frantically blew her whistle, which only attracted the elk's attention. Fortunately, both animals carried on and she could hear them crashing through the trees.

When Linda asked me why I had not responded to the whistle, I told her that I had thought it was a wild turkey. She was not pleased to have been considered a turkey. But all's well that ends well and hopefully our adventure can be repeated sometime—maybe with just a little less drama.

Chapter 62

Awakened

I was part of a most interesting prayer experiment a few years ago. Several of us had decided to see what would happen if we told the Lord that we were willing to step out of our comfort zones and share our faith. We agreed that we would examine our hearts and ask God to help us change areas that needed changing. And we asked for an infusion of courage and wisdom as we watched for opportunities to live and speak our beliefs.

We decided to share our experiences only with each other, exactly as they occurred, pleasant or unpleasant. We would then evaluate to see if the church at large could benefit from what we had learned. I thought that perhaps God would cause our paths to cross with people who needed to hear the good news of salvation but I did not really know what to expect.

I was most surprised to be awakened one morning with a name pounding in my head and I found myself repeating the name when my eyes opened. I sensed that I was supposed to visit and encourage some friends who had not attended church for many years. Although they had once been active and vibrant members they appeared to have lost their first enthusiasm and their lifestyle signaled a departure from their former spiritual and philosophical values.

My wife was still asleep but as soon as she stirred I told her what had transpired. I was apprehensive about my mission because I would be entering some very personal and private space. As the day progressed I wondered if perhaps my imagination was playing tricks on me.

At our midweek prayer service that evening, I asked my pastor how one would know if God was leading in a particular assignment. When I told him of my experience he said, "That is very interesting, just this morning I too, woke with a name that I feel compelled to visit." We agreed to compare notes when our visits were completed.

Several days later, a friend (I'll call him Rob) stopped by and asked if I could recommend an encouraging book of a spiritual nature that would be good for sharing with someone he had in mind. I gave him "Incredible Answers to Prayer" by Roger Morneau and said that I had not found anyone who had been offended by the book but many who had been so thankful and some who even considered the book to have been a lifesaver. And I added that I was beginning to see for myself some of the unbelievable things that Roger talked about.

As I went to my bookshelf I gave some quick reflection as to whether or not I should tell Rob about my most recent experience. Then I told him about my waking from a sound sleep with a definite sense of mission. I added that I had questioned my imagination until I talked to the pastor but that I still had reservations. I encouraged Rob to pass his book on and tell me what happened and I said that I would report back to him also. Then I laughingly told him that I realized I was getting myself into some kind of no-man's land by telling him about the experiment—it would be incomplete unless I actually followed through and I freely admitted that I was dragging my feet.

I was apprehensive because the kind of visit I felt impressed to do was of a very personal nature and I did not want to "meddle." I thought and thought, prayed and prayed and did nothing. Then I remembered the people who were waiting for my report. There was the prayer team (a support group of four, including the pastor) my wife (who supported from a safe distance) and Rob.

One night I drove to the people's house—well, not *to* the house exactly, but rather *by* the house. In fact I drove *by* the house several times. I wanted to make sure that there would be no other visitors and that my timing would be as good as possible. Then I just turned into the driveway, wondering what on earth I had gotten myself into.

Mrs. Jones met me at the door and we talked for what seemed like an eternity before I was able to escape. Mrs Jones did not invite me in and I did not tell her the real reason for my visit. I had previously decided that I would not launch into personal areas on the first visit, so I offered her the little "Incredible Answers to Prayer" book and a video. I told her about some experiences with the book. Then I left, feeling relieved, while I wondered what she must be thinking.

I had just entered the safety of my own home, when the phone rang. It was Rob's mother and she was chuckling. She said "I had to call you Murray to give you some encouragement." She explained that Mrs. Jones had just phoned her to say, "You will never guess who just stopped by. Murray came to the house and we had the most wonderful visit at the door. He gave me a book and a video and I'm going to watch the video right now."

Rob's mom further explained that Rob was at that very moment sitting in her living room. He had picked up only half of the telephone conversation but it had been enough to make him realize that I had followed through with my commitment. Then he had related my story to her, which is when she called me.

She said that Mrs. Jones had been on her special prayer list. She was very aware of the lifestyle changes and had been concerned. Because they were such close friends, she had not wanted to jeopardize the relationship and had been praying that God would intervene.

I hung up the phone with a sense of awe. How does it work? A woman prays, without knowledge of a support group that is trying to grow in faith. One of the participants is awakened and shares his experience with a man who also needs encouraging. That man happens to be in the right place at the right time and all parties have their needs met by an all-powerful God who makes it seem so easy.

Later, I also visited Mr. Jones and prayed with him. When he and his wife moved to another town, I wrote to them everything that was on my heart and told them of this experience and how a loving Father in heaven had reached down to touch all of us at the same time and how we needed to get serious. I encouraged them to find a church and start again.

It was many months later that I was talking to a relative of the Jones family. Out of the blue, he said that he had read my correspondence. Gulp. "What?" I asked. "I read what you wrote to my in-laws and it really has them thinking. Nothing like this has ever happened to them before. I want to talk to you some more about these things."

Another life was touched. We *have* talked more about these things and shared together and encouraged each other. The great God of the universe takes our tiny steps of trepidation and keeps them going by His power to create faith that is real and lasting. That faith is an essential part of a heavenly relationship that grows right into eternity.

Chapter 63

The Great Flood

My daughter completed her Biology degree and went on to become a pediatrician. In the process of her education, her beliefs were challenged as I said they would be. As she advanced in learning I would question her occasionally on her fundamentals. And although she studied different ways of viewing life, the complexity of the things she was learning convinced her more than ever of the evidence for a master designer.

It seems such a short time ago that she was asking me for assistance with some of her school projects. I still remember the day she came with a special question. She wanted to do a project for the "Science Fair" that was unique and different.

I suggested that she do a project on the world's great "flood." She replied, "Dad, this is a *science* project." I said, "Yeah, so? Don't you believe in the flood story?" Her reply was not totally convincing.

I told her that the flood story was the most widely told story around the world and that she could introduce her subject by interviewing local Natives to get their stories. I assured her that the stories were available and that the science was more impressive than she realized. I said that we could get books and videos and contact reputable scientists (some who still teach evolutionary theory) but believe in the biblical Creation and Flood stories.

Her grade 7/8 science project was titled "The Great Flood / Fact or Fiction?" I still enjoy reading her paper and smiling as I remember the fun we had as we gathered material. The simple information that follows comes pretty much directly from her project.

According to the Bible the whole world was once destroyed by water. It will be destroyed once again—this time by fire. Peter says, "First of all, you must understand that in the last days scoffers will come, scoffing and following their own evil desires, they will say, "Where is this coming he promised? Ever since our fathers died, everything goes on as it has since the beginning of creation." But they deliberately forget that long ago by God's word the heavens existed and the earth was formed out of water and by water. By these waters also the world of that time was deluged and destroyed. By the same word the present heavens and earth are reserved for fire, being kept for the day of judgment and destruction of ungodly men" (2 Peter 3:3-7, NIV).

The Bible tells the flood story right after giving a genealogical list complete with lifespan of patriarchs who lived up to that point. The story is told in the same manner—as a fact of history. Here are some of the basics of the story as recorded:

"The Lord then said to Noah, "Go into the ark you and your whole family, because I have found you righteous in this generation. Seven days from now I will send rain on the earth for forty days and forty nights, and I will wipe from the face of the earth every living creature I have made.

"In the six hundredth year of Noah's life, on the seventeenth day of the second month - on that day all the springs of the great deep burst forth, and the floodgates of the heavens were opened. And rain fell on the earth forty days and forty nights.

"For forty days the flood kept coming on the earth, and as the waters increased they lifted the ark high above the earth. The waters rose and increased greatly on the earth, and the ark floated on the surface of the water. They rose greatly on the earth, and all the high mountains under the entire heavens were covered. The waters rose and covered the mountains to a depth of more than twenty feet. Every living thing that moved on the earth perished - birds, livestock, wild animals, all the creatures that swarm over the earth, and all mankind.

"Everything on dry land that had the breath of life in its nostrils died. Every living thing on the face of earth was wiped out; men and animals and the creatures that move along the ground and the birds of the air were wiped from the earth. Only Noah was left, and those with him in the ark. The waters flooded the earth for a hundred and fifty days" (Gen. 7:1-24, NIV).

Civilizations throughout the world have stories of a great flood from long ago. Many of these legends are similar to the Bible story. They usually tell of the whole world being affected by water, with only a few people surviving. Nearly all the animals die and often boats or canoes are used for survival.

We talked to a local Native lady, Sarah Sampare, whose ancestors were from Hope Island—north of Port Hardy. The story passed down through generations tells of a voice that told her ancestors about the great flood to come. They found a cave, rolled a rock to the entrance and sealed it with a sticky substance from the trees.

John Charlie's people, originally from Blunden Harbour, were warned of the flood by a heavenly being. They were instructed to tie all their canoes together and go out to sea. While they were headed for the tallest mountain on the mainland shore, one canoe broke away. It drifted north, eventually arriving in the area of Kitimat. That is why there is a tribe in Kitimat that speaks a similar dialect.

Henry George showed us a video of opening ceremonies from the 1994 Commonwealth games in Victoria. In that video, a Native chief recounted the oral history from the coast mentioning many key events that continued back, back, back—to the time of the great flood.

"A flood legend from an Alaskan Indian tribe is as follows: Long ago the father of the Indian tribe lived toward the rising sun. He was warned in a dream that a great flood was coming, so he built a raft. On this raft he saved himself, his family, and all the animals. He floated for several months on the water. The animals on the raft complained. When a new land finally appeared, the animals, as punishment for their complaining, had lost the ability to talk" (*Earth Story,* p. 146).

We visited the Ginkgo Petrified Forest in Washington State. Although this area is now a desert region, it once had a lush semi-tropical climate. Over two hundred species of petrified logs have been identified here. This area was once under water as was much of the whole inland United States.

Cephalopods, giant oysters and clams have been found with the wood. Thus this area is identified with sea water. A giant flood is a possibility. The strata bordering the sides of the Columbia River may have been carved out when the layers were soft. The layers are flat with even contact and only the top shows signs of erosion. As with so many deposits of this kind, marine organisms are almost always found. Other petrified forests, depicted on a map, give evidence of vast water related deposits.

Trees are often found lying in the same direction as if deposited by water. Trees that are found upright usually have no bark, no limbs, and broken roots. As well, they often protrude through strata layers supposedly representing millions of years. No trees can normally last that long while sediments cover them over. So there was some kind of catastrophe and rapid sedimentation. Many geologists recognize vast local flooding but cannot fathom a flood of global proportions.

The Mount Saint Helen's volcanic explosion deposited 19,500 upright trees in Spirit Lake. It made instant canyons and strata layers. The trees had no bark, no limbs, and the roots were broken. The downed trees were mostly configured in one direction as they were deposited by the resulting slide and flood from melting snow.

Robert F. Correia, an amateur paleontologist and author of several papers, helped us gather this general information:

- Either marine or fresh water deposits for dinosaurian remains are the rule rather than the exception.

- Non-marine deposits invariably have their marine equivalent and appear above or below the other according to whether the sea was encroaching or receding from the land mass during the occasion of their deposition.

- Massive bone beds show signs of being tossed about and deposited like driftwood.

- Bones show rounded edges and abrasion.

- Brachiosaurus, the largest dinosaur was found covered with sea shells.

- Death positions often show possible death by drowning.

182

- Dinosaur tracks are found in sediment containing raindrop impressions and ripple marks. Amazing raindrop impressions are even found in the tracks themselves.

- Ankylosaurus, a top-heavy armord dinosaur is always found upside down, as are most armored dinosaurs.

Lisa's paper has a little section that says simply, "Other Points from books and videos:

- Present rates of erosion give evidence of a very young earth. Delta deposits at the mouths of all the world's major rivers are young—only several thousand years old. This would appear to agree with the timing of the biblical flood.

- Underwater turbidities (mud slides) explain rapid covering and fossil formation.

- Our area has many limestone caves which could have formed rapidly when the material was soft. Stalactites and stalagmites would have grown quickly with the mineralized water. It doesn't have to take millions of years. In fact, stalactites can be found under modern bridges when conditions are right.

- Fossils require quick burial but dinosaurs are large. A flood, with massive mud and sediment solves this problem.

- If mud is allowed to dry it will crack. Surprisingly, there is massive evidence of mud cracks in rocks.

- Bodies of animals are often found facing the same direction. This could be because they were deposited by water, like the fish in our boat hatches (all heads pointing up).

- Most dinosaur tracks proceed uphill. Were they escaping from water? If the layers show simple to complex it may be because some have the ability to move faster.

There were two things about the project that struck me as interesting. The first magazine that Lisa stumbled upon in her little school's library (100 students) turned out to be exactly what we were looking for. And later, the two judges who examined her project happened to be geologists who worked for the BHP Island Copper Mine which was still operating at the time. And they certainly were not Creationists.

It seemed so unusual that I later asked the principal if he had chosen them on purpose but he said that it had just happened as part of a random process. At the time, Lisa actually phoned me to ask what she should say. I told her that since this was a "science" project, all she was asked to do was to present her evidence. Before I tell you what the geologists said, I want to give you a few quotations from the little science magazine.

The article was titled "Earth's First Steps: Footprints From The Dawn Of Time," and it was written by Jerry Paul McDonald. He says, "I learned that marine fossils are common in the Robledos, but that footprints and plants were relatively rare. Anybody could find marine fossils... As I walked the Robledos, I hunted for the kind of rock that would produce fossil tracks. Much of the red sandstone material was so heavily rippled that footprints could never have formed. Strong ripples indicated a water energy much too great to allow preservation of footprints" (*Science Probe*, July 1992, p. 36, 37).

He says further, "The Robledo discovery gives us our best-known shot at interpreting an ancient terrestrial ecosystem. Literally a complete encyclopedia can be read.

"Under the headings "weather" and "climate,' we have etched into stone frequent raindrops, water and wind ripples, mud cracks from times of drought, and periodic dust storms and windstorms. There are also indications of tidal surges and retreats, small movements of the shoreline, and the formation of channels and drainage" (Ibid., p. 43).

Bones were also found. "Though not Permian in age, the bones represent an amazing variety of animals—including mastodon (elephant), rhinoceros, zebra/horse, wolf/dog, elk and deer, camel, bird, pig, bovine and at least three species of giant tortoise" (Ibid., p. 44).

Another section reads, "Trackway preservation is considered to be one of the rarest and least understood processes of fossilization. A number of very specific conditions have to be in place for trackway preservation to take place. Of the trillions of steps that are presently made by animals around the world in one day, the chance of a single print surviving the forces of nature for even a short time is remote" (Ibid., p. 45).

184

At the end of Lisa's paper is the response from the geologists (her critics). They said her material was new and interesting and that they had never previously considered the evidence her project presented; however, they still respectfully disagreed with her conclusion. But she was happy—her science project received a silver medallion.

Two of the people who told their legends have now died. Sarah Sampare is an old lady who is still a joy to talk to. I will summarize a letter I wrote to her some time back. She said that she thought my paper column was wonderful and that I should keep telling these kinds of stories. Therefore she will definitely get one of the first books.

"Hi, Sarah, when my daughter did a science project many years ago, we talked to you and several others to get some of the flood stories that have been passed down through the families. It was very interesting to see how the stories told around the world all have some common themes to the Bible story. Our history cannot be that old because the stories have not changed enough and are found everywhere throughout the world. The story in Genesis of how God confounded people's language and dispersed them throughout the world is the explanation I believe to be true even though it seems so wild to our modern way of thinking. Other modern explanations for these stories are even harder for me to believe.

"As far as we can tell by Bible dating and genealogy lists, we have only been here for about 6,000 years since Creation. I thought you might find some of the simple and practical evidences that we found for verification of the flood story to be interesting. There are lots of fossils in our area and fossils and petrified wood take water action and the tremendous amount of fossils throughout the world plus coal and oil which was buried by the flood and upheaval gives evidence of something huge that happened in the past.

"The Sasquatch stories are another area that I once laughed at but so many of my friends have had experiences with them that I am not laughing anymore. I have not categorized all the stories yet or written them out but you can see some of what I have. When I combine the pieces with the Native spiritual connection, I am coming to the belief that this is not an actual creature of the forest but rather in the spiritual realm. So it may be part of the deception that Satan plays on all humankind, especially if there is a link to belief in life after death which is not biblical."

"You might enjoy the water witching article too. Something that really fascinates me is that so many of the Native stories still tell like the Bible stories even though there has been so much mixing with the stories of the world. Many of the Natives knew that there was only one true Creator and some knew about the weekly Sabbath of creation that came every seventh day. Anyway I am still researching but find it sad that as the old generation passes away, so do the stories."

There are many internet sites (i.e. www.creationism.org) and a recent book Dinosaurs—An Adventist View *by David Read that will definitely challenge traditional thinking in the area of origins, flood and geology.*

Chapter 64

The Myth of a Progressive Faith

This article was written by Clifford Goldstein for *Signs of the Times* magazine in September 2001. It is reprinted here with permission. "According to a front-page bleep in the Washington Post, scientists have just determined the order of all 34 million chemical "letters" that spell out the genetic code for a single human chromosome.

"Now maybe my neural paths are hopelessly overgrown with tendrils of biblical creationism, but something about 34 million chemical letters on a *single* human chromosome (not to mention the 1.6 billion letters on all 46 chromosomes—*per cell!*) speaks to me—not about science or even about genetics, but about mythology.

"Nobody, of course, *believes*—present tense—in myths. The ancient Egyptians didn't build massive pyramids because of myths about life after death. They *believed* their stories. The Incas didn't tear out their children's hearts for *myths* about angry gods. They *believed* their stories. And millions today haven't rejected biblical creation for myths about natural selection, macroevolution, and survival of the fittest. They *believe* their stories.

"Myths are not what we believe. They are, instead, what becomes of what we once believed that we *no longer* believe. Truth, on the other hand, is what remains even after we stop believing it.

"Facts like 34 million pieces of information on a *single* human chromosome (and others like it) make me wonder how soon until evolution is demoted—as were Quetzalcoatl, the Egyptian underworld, and Zeus—to myth? Physicist Roger Penrose, hardly a biblical creationist, said that the odds against an ordered universe like ours developing at random is 1 in 10 to the 10th to the 30th power (a number far larger than the number of atomic *particles* believed to exist in the known universe). Obviously, then, the Rom. had more logical reasons to believe in the birth of Minerva from the brains of Jupiter than our contemporaries do in the birth of humanity from Darwin's mutation and natural selections.

"What tale, for example, do evolutionists tell about the human heart, which pumps life-giving blood to the body's 120 trillion cells? Remember, the heart can't work for more than a few minutes without that blood supplying its own needs; when the blood stops, so does the heart, right? So, how did the heart survive all those long, cold millions of years before blood finally evolved into something that could keep the heart alive so the heart could pump blood to itself?

"Not only can the heart not exist without blood, but blood can't exist without the heart: The heart pumps blood to the bones, which make red blood cells, and red blood cells feed the heart the oxygen it needs to survive. The question is, how did the bones exist all those millions of years before finally evolving into a factory for red blood cells—when bones themselves need the red blood cells to exist? *Bones can't exist without the very thing they themselves manufacture.* One needs a myth more incredible than Minerva's birth to explain how something creates the very thing that it needs to exist.

"We have that myth. It's called evolution.

187

"The incredible thing about myths, however, is the readiness with which people believe them. Some Christians exhibit a "progressive faith" by incorporating evolution into their, ahem, Christianity. Biblical history is replete with the fruit of such "progressive faith." Ancient Israel "progressed" past Moses and the prophets—right to myths of Baal, Moloch, Greek dualism (immortality of the soul), and, eventually, Roman sun worship. Those who meld the myth of evolution with the faith of Jesus are, in fact, nothing but twentieth-century versions of the ancient Israelites who mixed their children's blood with their sin offerings to Yahweh.

"We all need to believe in something. Some choose evolution as the source of those 34 million bits of information *per chromosome;* some choose Jesus, who—according to God's Word—created humans in a day.

"The biggest myth, however, is to think that you can choose both."

Chapter 65

Prophecy Code

Art historians recognize a universal language around the world consisting of colors, numbers and art forms. The color green represents life, and orange or gold are colors for the sun - as life giver. I briefly mentioned numbers already and gave 666 as an example. There is the circle of life and there are death boats, winged serpents and dragons found throughout the world.

When you understand the code you also understand the message and the story of the world is told in symbol. It can get very complex but there are basics that can be readily understood. The Bible also uses code language throughout but especially in certain specific books.

The Bible introduces beasts that we might not understand but from other sections of the Bible we get the keys to the code. For example, a beast is a benign symbol in and of itself and simply designates a kingdom (Dan. 7:17, 23). Some of the symbols would have been well known to the people to whom the messages were written. We also use symbols - including beasts, similarly.

Many years ago I was explaining this concept in a Revelation seminar. I knew that there were some Americans in the group so I said, "The tenacious donkey hopes that the pompous elephant will become mired in Iranian mud." The Canadians looked blank but the Americans broke into big smiles. You have to understand that the Iran Contra scandal was big news at that time. Reagan was president and an elephant is symbolic of the Republican Party while a donkey represents the Democrats.

Then I used an example for the Canadians. I continued, "The dogwood blossom sometimes feels overlooked and ignored by the larger maple leaf." Some looked puzzled until they remembered that the Pacific dogwood is British Columbia's floral emblem and the nation is represented by the maple leaf.

It is interesting that the book of the Apocalypse or Revelation, the last book of the Bible, reveals by using code language. It draws on the symbolism and stories from other scriptures to tell the story of the past, present and future. At the heart of the story is Jesus, the lamb slain from the foundation of the world, who is also the lion of the tribe of Judah. He is the Word, and the son of man, but returns as King of Kings.

Jesus is the Prince who takes on the dragon and Jesus wins. Thus we get to see how the story ends. The book has seven angels, seven churches, seven seals, seven trumpets, seven plagues and the list goes on. The number seven is God's number and represents completeness.

In the Old Testament, the number seven is used over and over. The city of Jericho was captured after the Israelites marched around the city for seven days, led by seven priests with seven trumpets. On the seventh day they marched around the city seven times. Namaan was healed of leprosy after he dipped seven times in the Jordan River. And of course, the world was created in seven days and the seventh day was set aside as a perpetual Sabbath reminder. It goes on and on.

The last book of the Bible especially goes hand in hand with the book of Daniel in the Old Testament. Daniel looks forward to events, many of which are now past history.

In the days of Babylon, Nebuchadnezzar dreamed of an image with a head of gold, chest and arms of silver, belly and thighs of bronze, legs of iron, and feet of iron and clay. God showed Daniel, who showed the king, that these metals represented successive kingdoms ending with a stone that smashed the image and filled the whole earth. The stone is of divine origin because it is specifically mentioned that the stone is cut out without human hands.

To the king, all of this was bad news because it showed that his kingdom would end and not only that other kingdoms would come and go, but also that the final kingdom would be God's kingdom and that this God was the God that Israel served.

To the Hebrews, Daniel and his friends, and believers down through history, this has been incredible good news. As the predicted kingdoms have come and gone, believers past and present have taken courage that God was and is in control. Everything is on schedule and God knows what he's doing.

Because the rock strikes the toes and because we know we are living in the time of the toes, we know that God's kingdom is about to begin. And for us at this point in history, that is very good news. The pain and suffering of this awful experiment with sin on our earth is just about over. Our focus is on the rock.

There is no question about who the rock is. We are instructed to build on the rock, we are told that the rock is our fortress; the water of life came from the rock in the wilderness. And that rock was and is Christ (1 Cor. 10:3).

About 50 years after the time of Nebuchadnezzar's dream, Daniel was given a parallel dream consisting of a lion-like beast, a lopsided bear, a swift leopard, and a horrible beast that had ten horns paralleling the ten toes.

This time some extra details are added but the time sequence and events are the same. A little horn uproots three of the other horns and then we are given a fantastic judgment scene, which is good news because after the judgment, God's kingdom is set up and the little horn's power is destroyed.

We know that the little horn grows out of Rome. We know that this horn fights against God and God's people but just like in Nebuchadnezzar's dream, it is Christ the rock who conquers and restores. The horn power is "broken without hand." This implies that the Lord Himself will eventually destroy this power.

The good news is found in the rock and the judgment and is the primary focus of these prophecies and should be the great hope of the people who live in the time just before God's kingdom rules the earth.

In the book of Daniel, God's people are judged and punished, Nebuchadnezzar is judged and repents, Belshazzar is judged—weighed in the balances, and found wanting. Those "balances" were a familiar picture of one's life being weighed and judged at time of death. By the way, the name "Daniel" means God is our judge.

About two years after Daniel's first vision, Daniel has another vision where he sees a ram with two lopsided horns; then a goat that seemingly flies, attacks the ram, and destroys it. The large horn on the goat's forehead breaks off and four horns take its place, paralleling the four heads of the leopard in Daniel's previous vision. Then a little horn grows up out of one of the four winds and does all the terrible things that the other horn from Rome had also done.

Daniel is told specifically that the next event is the cleansing of the sanctuary after 2300 evenings and mornings and he is told further that the prophecy concerns the time of the end. The kingdoms of Media-Persia and Greece are mentioned by name in Gabriel's interpretation. Interestingly, Babylon is not mentioned at all.

This prophecy is all about the time of the end and the sanctuary. At the same time it parallels the previous prophecies, but in a very new and focused manner. The animals mentioned are clean animals that were used in the sanctuary service. And furthermore the goats were specifically used in the cleansing of the sanctuary Day of Atonement services known today as Yom Kippur.

Babylon was at the very end of its allotted time period and in God's eyes was as good as finished. Medo-Persia is the starting point for the prophecies of both Daniel 8 and Daniel 9. And Babylon destroyed the temple and had nothing to do with its restoration but the nation of Persia was responsible for the services being restored.

The nation of Rome is not mentioned as such, but in the previous prophecies Rome never really disappeared—it simply changed, and that was from within. In this new prophecy the focus is on Rome's change to the little horn power which became exceedingly great. This prophecy focuses on the sanctuary while it parallels the previous prophecies. The horn power fights against God himself and thus is the more important aspect rising out of Rome. And this horn power has much more to do with the real sanctuary service than did the old nation of imperial Rome.

The seminar that I referred to previously was conducted as an evening event in a classroom of the local High School. I was most startled, on the very first night, to see a notation on the chalkboard identifying the political power that superseded and grew out of the Roman Empire. Then I realized that there must have been a history class in that room earlier in the day. That political power has never disappeared although it received a deadly wound just as the Bible said it would.

One day I was explaining the Prophecy Code and we looked at how Satan, as serpent and dragon, leads the whole world astray (Rev. 12:9). We discovered that when prophecy talks about a woman, it is talking about a church or God's people (Jer. 6:2; 2 Cor. 11:2; Isa. 51:16, 62:5). We were reading Revelation 17 where a harlot woman is pictured as sitting upon many waters. Verse 15 explains that the waters are peoples, multitudes, nations and languages. In verse 3 the woman rides a beast and a beast represents a kingdom or nation. This woman is dressed in purple and scarlet and in verse 6 has been a persecuting power.

The woman sits on seven hills, has a cup in her hand, and she has a name—Mystery, Babylon the Great, the Mother of Harlots and Abominations of the Earth. Suddenly a lady gasped and put her hand over her mouth. Without any explanation from me, she said, "I know what this is talking about." That's the way it is with the Prophecy Code.

I am only scratching the surface of some exciting and sobering topics. It is not my purpose to go too deep but rather to introduce.

I have done that by telling my story in a variety of areas. If anyone wants more of the Prophecy Code I recommend a web site with that very name—Prophecy code. Doug Batchelor, of "Amazing Facts," has compiled a variety of study materials, amongst which, is a sheet that gives the keys to unlocking the symbols.

For the keys to the code, check www.prophecycode.com or www. BibleProphecyTruth.com and go to *"keys to Bible symbols."*

Also be sure to see or read Pastor Doug's personal story, *The Richest Caveman.*

Chapter 66

Not By Chance

A few years ago I took my father-in-law on a fishing and exploration expedition to Smith Inlet. I told him some of the stories that have been written in this book and I showed him some of the places I had lived as a boy. I also explained the winged serpent, sun worship and circle of life (representing the belief that life never ends).

I took him to a place that had once been

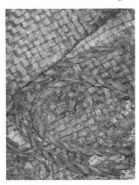

a Native burial site but had long since been pillaged and then reclaimed by nature. I knew that my mother had recognized the heritage value and had introduced the Native Band to anthropologists who preserved many of the artifacts. There had been cedar bark blankets, hats, and baskets as well as Hudson Bay trading blankets and beads. Now there was nothing.

The moss was about a foot thick and Harold, for no particular reason, bent over and pulled a thick chunk from the forest floor. I could not believe my eyes. There, on the ground, was a silver earring in the form of Sisiutl the serpent. It formed a circle - with its tail in its mouth. And when Harold pulled another chunk of moss he found the matching serpent. We also found a few pieces of cedar bark rope and cloth and after we removed the ingrown moss and lichens, they dried nicely.

Something similar happened when I visited Nepal recently. I was on a trip to check on some indigenous mission workers that my church sponsored through an organization called "Gospel Outreach." I had seen the snake charmers; serpent symbolism was everywhere and the ancient gods were openly worshipped. The stories I heard were frightening and almost unbelievable (too many to tell in this book).

At one point, I was asked to speak at a school. In the audience was a Hindu woman who had her child in the school and the tuition was paid by an American doctor ($50 per month). She was so thankful and was sitting with the mission group to see what they had to say. I was watching her as I spoke through an interpreter.

I told about the things I was seeing and learning and I talked about the serpent and what it meant. Then I told about the Bible's teaching and how Jesus gives freedom from ritual and freedom from fear. She was sitting on the edge of her seat and later there were many questions.

When my group went back to our hotel I was shocked to see something that I had previously missed. Above the entrance was a face (the god Shiva, I think) and leading from the open mouth, in opposite directions, was a double headed serpent and it had wings (I am curious now, to know if it faced east and west). Under the face were two winged dragons.

I had seen something similar in my home town. The Fort Rupert ceremonial longhouse has a face and a double headed serpent and the stories tell of its ability to fly. Out of all three mouths comes a frog— the transformer (remember the story of the frog that transforms into a prince?) The Nepalese people do not know about the Kwakiutl people of British Columbia. There is more here than meets the eye.

In previous stories I have quoted some verses from the Bible but let me do it again. "And the great dragon was cast out, that old serpent, called the Devil, and Satan, which deceiveth the whole world: he was cast out into the earth, and his angels were cast out with him" (Rev. 12:9). "And I saw three unclean spirits like frogs come out of the mouth of the dragon, and out of the mouth of the beast, and out of the mouth of the false prophet. For they are the spirits of devils, working miracles, which go forth unto the kings of the earth and of the whole world, to gather them to the battle of that great day of God Almighty (Rev. 16: 13, 14).

I don't think these experiences happened randomly by chance. I had just been thinking about and talking about the very things that were immediately verified. I have the artifacts and photos now to show what I am talking about. And I have given additional information for those who might wish to probe deeper.

My "Zeballos" story is true and so is my "Crisis of Faith" story. There are so many other stories that I could share but this book must come to a close. I have had direct answers to prayer. I have been awakened in the night and felt the presence of evil and also the incredible assurance that comes from knowing a loving God. Jesus turns no honest seeker away.

Millions of people know exactly what I'm talking about. There is a God in heaven who knows all about us and He brings events into our lives that are designed to get our attention. I am beginning to think that nothing is by chance. The Bible says that all things work together for good, to them that love the Lord. Maybe it is not by chance that you are reading this book.

Chapter 67

Tricks That Aren't So Funny

When I was a boy we took some relatives for an excursion on the boat. One of my cousins saw me at the sink, filling a cup with water. She did not know that my foot was operating a switch on the floor to make the faucet work. I told her that if you simply waved at the faucet it would spout water.

She knew that could not be true but I told her to try it for herself (I kept my foot placed strategically over the switch). Those who knew what was going on played along and waved as if that was normal procedure. Eventually my cousin tried it and it worked for her too. She was now a believer because she had seen it with her own eyes.

I could have told her that she needed to harness the power within and visualize the water coming from the faucet. That also would have appeared plausible but it would have been a trick.

I was once watching a live television show for youth. On this particular day a psychic was explaining his gift and kids were invited to call-in with questions. One boy had lost an item and another had been missing his dog for several days.

The psychic told the first boy to look under some objects in a certain corner of his bedroom. He told the other boy to go quickly to a certain park and look in a specific area to find his dog. Before the program was over, both boys called back and excitedly and thankfully confirmed the psychic's information.

Then a hypnotist was brought on stage and he was working with a volunteer from the audience. The audience was watching closely but suddenly and without warning, the hypnotist said that everyone in the studio was going to feel a pinch. All the people screamed, jumped out of their seats, and turned in unison to see who had pinched their backsides. Of course there was no-one there—at least no-one who could be seen.

I did not laugh; in fact I wondered if I should even be watching the show. I would never physically participate in anything like that. We are told by hypnotists that it is all the power of suggestion. But what if all those people really were pinched? I know that may seem like an impossible idea but there are countless stories of people whose lives have been overtaken by some strange occult force after participating in such experiments.

Hypnotism was once called animal magnetism and mesmerism. Franz Anton Mesmer is considered to be the father of hypnotism. He was also an astrologer. Hypnotism is the submitting of one's mind to another. That should never, never be allowed and I submit that it can result in the takeover of one's mind by Satanic forces. Most hypnotists, themselves, do not understand what they are dealing with.

Channelers and psychics sometimes explain their ability as a natural gift of birth. Others claim to be able to tap the inner power or the universal energy etc. Some claim to receive messages from the dead and others say that they converse with angels. Some use tricks of their own but many are, themselves, deceived by outside forces. All use methods that are condemned in the Bible.

There are those who know exactly what they are doing and have made a conscious choice. Roger Morneau, in his book, *Trip Into the Supernatural*, tells how he met people in high places who knowingly worshipped Lucifer and received great monetary wealth as a result. They worshipped powerful and majestic beings who materialized and their pictures were on the walls of the worship center.

The members of this secret society laughed at people who attended séances to talk to the dead. They knew that Satan and his angels were tricking them but they didn't care. They lived for the moment and they believed Satan to be so powerful that he would ultimately win in the war against the biblical God and they intended to be on the winning side. Roger tells how the true God rescued him from this group.

My wife has a friend who excitedly told her about an experience with a psychic. She, with some other women, had hired a psychic to come to her home. When her turn came for a session, she entered a room where all the windows were closed. Although there was no fan in the room, a soothing, cool breeze blew on her face.

197

My wife told her that she should be careful and explained some of the things I have been writing about. Her friend was intelligent and well educated and she said, "You don't believe *that* do you?" Although she did not understand the strange phenomenon, she thought that Linda's explanation was absolutely ridiculous.

We have another friend who prays to a presence who manifests himself in the form of a white light. She believes it to be the "Christ Spirit" and says it (he) is wonderful and good. She knows there are evil spirits and practices *white* witchcraft in opposition to *black* witchcraft with its spells and curses. She even has a photo of the white light and offered to do a demonstration. She did not seem offended when we respectfully declined.

This woman is also a healer and people come to her for help with physical and emotional problems. She believes herself to be reincarnated and has experienced some amazing dreams regarding her past and she has been able to verify the places and events from her dreams. She is also able to do something she calls "astral travel" which allows her to see real things, in distant places, in real time.

Here is a woman who has proof for what she believes - and that is her reality. We explained that, according to the Bible, all witchcraft is from the enemy even if it produces helpful results. Satan is called an angel of light (2 Cor. 11:14) and his original name, Lucifer, means light-bearer. She began to literally tremble but still wanted to hear what the Bible teaches about death because her dad had visited her 3 times after he died and once even sat on her bed.

Jesus wants us to know the truth and if we will read His instruction and get to know Him, He will make the trickery stop. It was Jesus who promised that we could know the truth and that the truth would set us free (John 8:32).

If it suits his purposes, Satan can reveal himself openly. If some choose not to believe that he exists, that is okay too. He does not mind that he is pictured as a freak with horns and a long tail. He is a master at adapting to every society and type of person. He can function quite nicely within a church. It is only essential that people not literally get to know and put their trust in the real Savior.

I believe that Harry Potter books and television magic shows of all types are setting us up for the real thing. Some people, who should know better, are reading the books to their kids for educational purposes. But as I told one lady, I would not read pornography to my kids, lest in the process the story should become too enchanting.

I have a very good book called *The Mainstreaming of New Age* by Manuel Vasquez. It was given to me by a friend who became very disturbed by the book. Rhonda said that she was almost overcome with an irrational desire to rip the book to shreds. Then she analyzed her feelings and came to a shocking conclusion.

She had been trained in psychology and family counseling and had picked up some tools and methodologies that the book warned against. She told how she had seen three slight women lift a large man in a sofa chair—using only two fingers. It appeared effortless and was supposed to be an example of mind over matter when positive energy was channeled.

Rhonda realized that her university had been unwittingly teaching occult methodologies as if they were scientific. There was a spiritual battle raging in her mind and her thinking changed (paradigm shifts can be difficult). That is when she gave the book to me.

Every aspect of our society is being infiltrated with ancient spiritualistic modalities. Manuel Vasquez mentions energy manipulation with its acupuncture, acupressure, Shiatsu, therapeutic touch and reflexology. And there is yoga, transcendental meditation, guided imagery, visualization, biofeedback, hypnosis, pendulum divination, applied kinesiology, iridology, aura readings, channeling, psychic healing, chakra balancing, homeopathy and aromatherapy (*The Mainstreaming of New Age*, pp. 122, 123).

So-called "universal healing energy" has many different names in various cultures. Some of these names are chi, prana, pneuma, mana, orenda etc. "Acupressure is Chinese, shiatsu is Japanese, and reflexology is a Western variety of energy-balancing techniques. Though the massage techniques in the various therapies may vary, the idea that the therapy manipulates the flow of energy comes from the same source" (Ibid., p. 138).

The *Alternative Health Dictionary* lists several thousand names for various therapies that use energy balancing. For Christians, Mr. Vasquez advocates a "three strikes" principle. First, they are based on non-biblical worldviews. Second, their pioneers were into the occult. Third, they are an abomination to God. They are out! (Ibid., p. 181).

Therapeutic touch is a therapy that goes beyond normal massage for sore muscles. The book *Spiritualistic Deceptions in Health and Healing,* written by Dr. Edwin Noyes reports that "the originator of this type of energy medicine is Dora Kunz, president of the Theosophical Society, 1975 to 1987. Dora Kunz is herself a spiritualist who looks to invisible intelligences, angels and theosophy's ascended Masters for inspiration and guidance.'

"'Delores Krieger credits Dora Kunz for her knowledge of this practice. Krieger also had additional training in occult healing techniques. She studied yoga, Ayurvedic medicine (Hindu occultism applied to medicine), occultic Tibetan medicine, and Chinese traditional medicine. Delores Krieger has been a leading promoter of therapeutic touch in the nursing profession" (p. 138).

Dr. Edwin Noyes studied alternative healing methods for 20 years before he was ready to make a definitive statement. The book is well researched and very thorough. I am so thankful for books like this one - which expose Satan's tricks. These tricks are sophisticated and have eternal consequences and they should be taken very, very seriously.

Chapter 68

"If"

Will Baron was a man who decided to take God's promises to heart. He read and claimed Jesus' instruction, "Therefore I tell you, whatever you ask for in prayer, believe that you have received it, and it will be yours" (Mark 11:24, NIV). As he and his friends studied their Bibles and prayed together, they also claimed this promise, "And I will do whatever you ask in my name, so that the Son may bring glory to the Father. You may ask me for anything in my name, and I will do it" (John 14:13, 14, NIV).

Amazing things began to happen. He was personally directed by a living power and began preaching and witnessing at the beach and on the street. It was miraculous and often a voice spoke in his head directing him to specific activities. But eventually, so many demands were made on his time that he cursed the name of Jesus. Then he found, to his horror, that it had not been Jesus at all but rather that angel, Satan, who masquerades as "an angel of light" (2 Cor. 11:14) and seeks "...to deceive even the elect—if that were possible" (Matt. 24:24). Will tells the horrifying story in his book, *Deceived by the New Age*.

What is our protection against deception? The warnings that Jesus gave are for us; in fact, Jesus was talking to believers when he said these words, "Not every one that saith unto me, Lord, Lord, shall enter into the kingdom of heaven; but he that doeth the will of my Father which is in heaven. Many will say to me in that day, Lord, Lord, have we not prophesied in thy name? and in thy name have cast out devils? and in thy name done many wonderful works? And then will I profess unto them, I never knew you: depart from me, ye that work iniquity" (Matt. 7:21-23). That word "iniquity" refers to those who do not obey God's law. But they thought that they "knew" God and that He was working miracles and answering their prayers mightily.

Knowing Jesus is all tied up with obedience, "For whosoever shall do the will of my Father which is in heaven, the same is my brother, and sister, and mother" (Matt. 12:50). "If ye love me, keep my commandments. . . . He that hath my commandments, and keepeth them, he it is that loveth me: and he that loveth me shall be loved of my Father, and I will love him, and will manifest myself to him" (John 14:15, 21). "And hereby we do know that we know him, if we keep his commandments. He that saith, I know him, and keepeth not his commandments, is a liar, and the truth is not in him. But whoso keepeth his word, in him verily is the love of God perfected: hereby know we that we are in him. He that saith he abideth in him ought himself also so to walk, even as he walked" (1 John 2:3-6). "Whosoever committeth sin transgresseth also the law: for sin is the transgression of the law. And ye know that he was manifested to take away our sins; and in him is no sin. Whosoever abideth in him sinneth not: whosoever sinneth hath not seen him, neither known him" (1 John 3:4-6). "For this is the love of God, that we keep his commandments: and his commandments are not grievous" (1 John 5:3).

Daniel knew God and we can read his great prayer of supplication. He pleaded with God and fasted in sackcloth and ashes. He tells us, "And I prayed unto the LORD my God, and made my confession, and said, O Lord, the great and dreadful God, keeping the covenant and mercy to them that love him, and to them that keep his commandments; We have sinned, and have committed iniquity, and have done wickedly, and have rebelled, even by departing from thy precepts and from thy judgments. Yea, all Israel have transgressed thy law, even by departing, that they might not obey thy voice; therefore the curse is poured upon us, and the oath that is written in the law of Moses the servant of God, because we have sinned against him" (Dan. 9:4, 5, 11). He ends, "O my God, incline thine ear, and hear; open thine eyes, and behold our desolations, and the city which is called by thy name: for we do not present our supplications before thee for our righteousnesses, but for thy great mercies. O Lord, hear; O Lord, forgive; O Lord, hearken and do; defer not, for thine own sake, O my God: for thy city and thy people are called by thy name" (Dan. 9:18, 19).

Moses was a great intercessor for his people and saved them from disaster more than once (Ex. 32:9-14, 32; Num. 14:11-20). Samuel was another tremendous intercessor who was recognized as such by Israel (1 Sam. 7:8, 9). He is the one who said, "Moreover as for me, God forbid that I should sin against the LORD in ceasing to pray for you: but I will teach you the good and the right way" (1 Sam. 12:23). It was probably these men who inspired Jeremiah to pray, "We acknowledge, O LORD, our wickedness, and the iniquity of our fathers: for we have sinned against thee. Do not abhor us, for thy name's sake, do not disgrace the throne of thy glory: remember, break not thy covenant with us. Are there any among the vanities of the Gentiles that can cause rain? or can the heavens give showers? art not thou he, O LORD our God? therefore we will wait upon thee: for thou hast made all these things" (Jer. 14:20-22).

In this case, God's response is shocking. "Then said the LORD unto me, Though Moses and Samuel stood before me, yet my mind could not be toward this people: cast them out of my sight, and let them go forth. And it shall come to pass, if they say unto thee, Whither shall we go forth? then thou shalt tell them, Thus saith the LORD; Such as are for death, to death; and such as are for the sword, to the sword; and such as are for the famine, to the famine; and such as are for the captivity, to the captivity" (Jer. 15:1, 2). For too long, the people had rejected the pleading of the Sovereign God.

It is the Holy Spirit that draws us, brings us to repentance, changes and empowers us. More than anything else, God wants our honesty. Paul says that he was shown mercy because he was ignorant. (1 Tim. 1:13). We are told, "And the times of this ignorance God winked at; but now commandeth all men every where to repent" (Acts 17:30). And Jesus said, "If I had not come and spoken to them, they would not be guilty of sin. Now, however, they have no excuse for their sin." (John 15:22, NIV).

There are serious consequences when we knowingly ignore God's instruction. "If I regard iniquity in my heart, the Lord will not hear me" (Ps. 66:18). "Behold, the LORD'S hand is not shortened, that it cannot save; neither his ear heavy, that it cannot hear: But your iniquities have separated between you and your God, and your sins have hid his face from you, that he will not hear" (Isa. 59:1, 2). Solomon tells us, "He that turneth away his ear from hearing the law, even his prayer shall be abomination" (Prov. 28:9). However, he goes on to say, "He that covereth his sins shall not prosper: but whoso confesseth and forsaketh them shall have mercy" (Prov. 28:13).

It is bad enough that our relationship with God can be so seriously compromised, but it is worse than that. Those people who hear the awful words, "Depart from me, I never knew you," thought that they had marvelous answers to prayer but they had been deceived. God's law is our wall of protection and a breach in that wall can let the flood waters in. That is why Isaiah admonishes, "And they that shall be of thee shall build the old waste places: thou shalt raise up the foundations of many generations; and thou shalt be called, The repairer of the breach, The restorer of paths to dwell in" (Isa. 58:12).

The sober reality is that Satan can take the place of God. Our obedience is our protection from deception and our guarantee that we are connecting with the right God. We need not fear because God promises, "For I know the thoughts that I think toward you, saith the LORD, thoughts of peace, and not of evil, to give you an expected end. Then shall ye call upon me, and ye shall go and pray unto me, and I will hearken unto you. And ye shall seek me, and find me, when ye shall search for me with all your heart" (Jer. 29:11-13).

One of the greatest prayers of all time is King Solomon's prayer of dedication for the temple. God heard and renewed His covenant with Israel. His words still ring true for us today: "If my people, which are called by my name, shall humble themselves, and pray, and seek my face, and turn from their wicked ways; then will I hear from heaven, and will forgive their sin, and will heal their land" (2 Chron. 7:14). Those words are our protection. Those words are our guarantee. What wonderful words of life.

Chapter 69

Who Is This Jesus?

Long ago some mariners were about to perish in a terrible storm. They watched a man named Jesus rebuke the storm by telling it to be quiet. The Bible says that the wind ceased and there was a great calm. The men's reaction is recorded; "And they feared exceedingly, and said one to another, what manner of man is this, that even the wind and the sea obey him?" (Mark 4:41).

He is called the "Word." "In the beginning was the Word, and the Word was with God, and the Word was God. The same was in the beginning with God. All things were made by him; and without him was not any thing made that was made" (John 1:1-3). "He was in the world, and the world was made by him, and the world knew him not. And the Word was made flesh, and dwelt among us, (and we beheld his glory, the glory as of the only begotten of the Father,) full of grace and truth" (John 1:10, 14).

I've proposed that at the core level of all religious thought, there are only two systems—and they meet at the cross. When we speak of the biblical God we also use the term Godhead because God is triune. This concept is found throughout the world because Lucifer (a created being) rebelled against his Creator and wanted to be worshipped just like God (Isa. 14:12-14). He is a copy artist, thief and liar. It is to his advantage to keep us in the dark regarding Jesus.

The Bible tells us that God is love. God does not force allegiance and the story of Jesus shows how far God will stretch to gain our trust. When our first parents decided to try it alone, our world became a test case and an example for the universe. But God did not cast us off. The Bible says, "For God so loved the world, that he gave his only begotten Son, that whosoever believeth in him should not perish, but have everlasting life" (John 3:16).

The Bible is also called the "Word" and it is the story of Jesus from beginning to end. When he came as a man he told the people, "Search the scriptures; for in them ye think ye have eternal life: and they are they which testify of me. And ye will not come to me, that ye might have life" (John 5:39, 40).

Jesus has a multitude of titles because as he testifies, "I am the Alpha and Omega, the beginning and the end, the first and the last" (Rev. 22:13). He shares the supreme names and titles for the eternal God. As the Word and communicator he was the LORD (Jehovah) who walked and talked with Adam and Eve. At times he thundered; other times he talked with a still, small voice.

The communicator has veiled God's glory so that men could exist in his presence. When his glory was partially revealed it was almost overwhelming. He came in the form of a man before his miraculous birth. Abraham met three men one day and he did not realize at first that two of the visitors were angels and one was the LORD (Gen. 18).

As the story unfolds, the two angels leave and the LORD remains to talk to Abraham. Then when Sodom is destroyed for its wickedness, there is this interesting verse: "Then the LORD rained upon Sodom and upon Gomorrah brimstone and fire from the LORD out of heaven" (Gen. 19:24).

Jesus as WORD and LORD would have spoken the Ten Commandments to the Israelites. These commands make up royal law of love and liberty - when correctly understood. And they are the only words that we have that were actually written by God himself—on stone (Ex. 31:18). They are foundational to lasting happiness.

These are the commandments written by God as found in Exodus 20:2-17:

1. I am the LORD thy God, which have brought thee out of the land of Egypt, out of the house of bondage. Thou shalt have no other gods before me.

2. Thou shalt not make unto thee any graven image, or any likeness of any thing that is in heaven above, or that is in the earth beneath, or that is in the water under the earth: Thou shalt not bow down thyself to them, nor serve them: for I the LORD thy God am a jealous God, visiting the iniquity of the fathers upon the children unto the third and fourth generation of them that hate me; And shewing mercy unto thousands of them that love me, and keep my commandments.

3. Thou shalt not take the name of the LORD thy God in vain; for the LORD will not hold him guiltless that taketh his name in vain.

4. Remember the sabbath day, to keep it holy. Six days shalt thou labour, and do all thy work: But the seventh day is the sabbath of the LORD thy God: in it thou shalt not do any work, thou, nor thy son, nor thy daughter, thy manservant, nor thy maidservant, nor thy cattle, nor thy stranger that is within thy gates: For in six days the LORD made heaven and earth, the sea, and all that in them is, and rested the seventh day: wherefore the LORD blessed the sabbath day, and hallowed it.

5. Honour thy father and thy mother: that thy days may be long upon the land which the LORD thy God giveth thee.

6. Thou shalt not kill.

7. Thou shalt not commit adultery.

8. Thou shalt not steal.

9. Thou shalt not bear false witness against thy neighbour.

10. Thou shalt not covet thy neighbour's house, thou shalt not covet thy neighbour's wife, nor his manservant, nor his maidservant, nor his ox, nor his ass, nor any thing that is thy neighbour's.

Satan caused the downfall of Adam and Eve and he used a beautiful talking serpent. This earth has become an awful example of what happens when we let him take control. Because love cannot be commanded, Jesus became our Redeemer—one of his titles. We must *choose* him because we *want* him.

Genesis 3:15 gives the promise of a Savior that was to come and the Bible tells that story throughout its pages. From time to time genealogy lists were given so that the promised *seed* could be traced. We were even told the literal kingdoms that would come and go in the process. And Daniel, hundreds of years in advance, gave the exact time that the Messiah (another title for Jesus) would arrive (Dan. 9).

The prophet Isaiah said of this promised Savior, "For unto us a child is born, unto us a son is given: and the government shall be upon his shoulder: and his name shall be called Wonderful, Counselor, The mighty God, The everlasting Father, The Prince of Peace" (Isa. 9:6). This is a verse often quoted during the Christmas season.

Isaiah is responsible for another familiar Christmas passage which says, "Therefore the Lord himself shall give you a sign; Behold, a virgin shall conceive, and bear a son, and shall call his name Immanuel" (Isa. 7:14). The word *Immanuel* means "God with us."

The Bible not only told us when Jesus would come and when he would be sacrificed for us; it also told us where he would be born and how he would live his life and what he would accomplish. And it tells us that Jesus is coming back as King of Kings and Lord of Lords. That time cannot be far off.

The New Testament is filled with stories of people who met Jesus and had their lives dramatically changed. Many accepted him as Lord and Savior while others rejected and hated him. The reasons for these reactions are explained.

It is not enough to know *about* Jesus; we are actually invited to get to know the real Jesus for ourselves. My faith is still growing. In that regard, I empathize with a desperate man who came to Jesus and said, "*If* you can do anything, please help me" (Mark 9). Jesus did not turn him away. He has not turned me away and he will not turn you away either. But don't play with him—this is serious business.

The story that I wrote called "My Crisis of Faith" took place while I was conducting a Revelation seminar. In that seminar I told the people, "At this point, I don't know you or what you believe, but it doesn't matter. We are going to treat the Bible on the same basis as any other book but see if it merits special status by the time we are finished." The participants were allowed to question and they could disagree as long as they disagreed agreeably.

I also encouraged them to try something that I considered vital and critical. "You may not know if there is a God," I said, "but pray to Him anyway. It can't hurt and the God of the Bible does not force anyone. He invites you to come, but unlike Satan, He will also let you go."

I even said that they could tell God that they wanted to find Him if He existed and that they wanted to find the *true* God. Amazing things happened and for some, there was quite a struggle. We all had our thinking challenged and some accepted Jesus as their friend and Savior.

I would give the same invitation to anyone who is reading this story. Your life can be given new meaning and relevance. You can know why you are here and where you are going. Spend time every day with the Word—He is the hope of the world.

I would suggest first spending some time with the gospels—Matthew, Mark, Luke, and John. Visit www.amazingfacts.org and www.3abn.org for assistance with further Bible studies and helpful resources.

Chapter 70

The Greatest Story Ever Told

A close friend once soberly, shared a story while it was still fresh—
and never mentioned it again. Anne worked with another woman and
knew her well—too well. She knew her faults and weaknesses and
sometimes the close contact produced conflict. But they also worshipped at the same church.

One particular day the members were sharing stories and testimo-
nies of the Lord's great love and power. Some shared prayer requests
and answers to previous prayer requests. And then her co-worker went
forward. As usual, she began weeping and carrying on and telling of
God's great goodness to her. Anne was disgusted and considered it to
be showmanship and theatrics. The real Joan was the Joan she knew
at work.

Anne vented her irritation at home and was still thinking about it
as she drove to work the next morning. Suddenly her thoughts became
confused and she panicked as she lost touch with her surroundings.
She found herself unable to think and she didn't know what she was
doing or where she was going.

She almost forgot her own name and she lost the ability to speak.
Then, very slowly, the words to a children's song came to her mind.
"Jesus loves me this I know, for the Bible tells me so. Little ones to
Him belong; they are weak but He is strong. Yes, Jesus loves me, yes
Jesus loves me…"

She began to hum, and then as her world became focused once
again, she started to sing. Anne shared her story without comment,
perhaps because the message was too painfully evident. And I have
not forgotten.

A church is a hospital for sick people and that is why there are a
lot of sick people in churches. Jesus invites all of us to come just as we
are but then he begins treating us. Some of us don't like the treatment.
Others of us don't like being in the presence of so many sick people.

My wife and I know from experience that the Lord can fix some very desperate situations. Perhaps another time we will share a story that comes from our favorite text. "This poor man cried, and the LORD heard him, and saved him out of all his troubles. The angel of the LORD encampeth round about them that fear him, and delivereth them. O taste and see that the LORD is good: blessed is the man that trusteth in him" (Ps. 34:6-8).

There is another passage that has great meaning for us. "Thou wilt keep him in perfect peace, whose mind is stayed on thee: because he trusteth in thee. Trust ye in the LORD for ever: for in the LORD JEHOVAH is everlasting strength" (Isa. 26:3, 4). Here also is a personal story for another time.

I remember when I became convinced that the Bible might contain the answers to our world's perplexing questions. I found that the Bible promises that the person who searches with all his heart will find God. And I began to feel a great sense of peace and assurance.

I had previously thought that if God did exist, He was unfair. I had not asked to be born and I had no power over my circumstances or struggle to find meaning. But I found that while one man (Adam) produced this mess, another man (Jesus) offers the free gift of salvation and righteousness. And He not only forgives; He also cleanses.

Jesus owned us but was forced to buy us back (redeem us) and the price was severe. The Bible promises hope and absolute acceptance. And thus, without question, the story of our salvation is the greatest story ever told.

Postscript

I have suggested that there are only two religious systems in the world. I would suggest further that none of us can escape the impact they have on every aspect of our lives. One of those systems has the Bible, a book that has often been banned, ridiculed, or said to be myth.

It seems to me that if the Bible is just a story book—a book of myth and imagination—then it should present no threat whatsoever. And it should at least be promoted as one of the great books of literature. But for some reason it has created more controversy than any other book ever produced. Maybe we should be asking why.

Many years ago I met an artist who had traveled the world and noticed a fascinating story told in art forms. He had a lecture that touched on the stories of winged serpents and dragons. He also mentioned a connection to UFOs, and he suggested that Satan may pull the greatest hoax in the history of the world by seeking to mimic Jesus' return.

For a world view that is more popular, go to the google search engine and try the words *crystalinks winged serpents and dragons*. Ellie Crystal claims to be guided by a spirit named Zoroaster—a name that has ancient anti-biblical connotations. Ellie has gathered a wealth of information with multiple links to other sources of information.

Ellie is a psychic and believes that she has a special calling and destiny. If you have read all my stories to this point you will understand why I advise caution. On the day that I viewed the Crystalinks Web site it claimed to have had 1,866,397 unique visitors the previous day. That's quite a few visitors.

Obviously the Crystalinks Web site does not share my worldview but it does have a tremendous amount of valuable information. Some other Web sites that do share my view and that also have a wealth of information—www.amazingfacts.org and www.3abn.org.

I have made reference to some interesting books that also do not share my conclusions. In regard to divining rods, perhaps the best book I have found is one called *The Art of Dowsing* by Richard Webster.

My friend John Bindernagel has tried to bring credibility to his Sasquatch book by consciously distancing himself from anything to do with the paranormal. His book *North America's Great Ape: The Sasquatch* is written within careful parameters. His Web site is www. bigfootbiologist.org.

The book *Indian Healing* by Wolfgang G. Jilek definitely goes counter to what I believe but I must admit—it is a riveting read. And then there is the book *Psychic Discoveries Behind the Iron Curtain* by Sheila Ostrander and Lynn Schroeder. Although published in the 1970s, its 457 pages are still hard to beat.

More on my side would be *Gods of the New Age* by Caryl Matrisciana, *The Evolution Conspiracy* by Caryl Matrisciana and Roger Oakland, and *The Dinosaur—An Adventist View.*

Living Lies About Death And The Hereafter is a book by Henry Feyerabend and it pictures a coiled snake on the front cover; so that combination should explain where it is coming from.

There are so many good books but I will sign off by listing just five more—*The Two Babylons, The Antichrist 666, Spiritualistic Deceptions In Health And Healing, The Mainstreaming of New Age, The Incredible Power of Prayer...* Good reading and God bless.

TEACH Services, Amazing Facts, ABC books, Hope TV, LLBN, and 3ABN are all further sources of information for those who might wish to dig a little deeper.

Acknowledgments

Chapter illustrations by Avalon Adventist
Academy Fifth and Sixth Grade students:

Page 2	Carlye Smedley
Page 4	FerrisCottreau
	Matthew McDonald
Page 6	Edan Oickle
Page 15	Shelby Smithson
Page 29	Chloe Cook
Page 31	Veronica Barnes
Page 35	Audrey Johnstone
Page 48	Darci Smith
Page 51	Foster Walkus
Page 59	Regan Dunlop
Page 68	Lauren Corsi
Page 72	Carlye Smedley

Image Credits

Page 151	Herb Roe, Artist
Page 154	Ken Knopp

We invite you to view the complete
selection of titles we publish at:

www.TEACHServices.com

Scan with your mobile
device to go directly
to our website.

Please write or email us your praises, reactions, or
thoughts about this or any other book we publish at:

info@TEACHServices.com

TEACH Services, Inc.
P U B L I S H I N G
11 Quartermaster Circle
Fort Oglethorpe, GA 30742

TEACH Services' titles may be purchased in bulk for
educational, business, fund-raising, or promotional use.
For more information, please e-mail:

BulkSales@TEACHServices.com

Finally, if you are interested in seeing
your own book in print, please contact us at:

publishing@TEACHServices.com

We would be happy to review your manuscript for free.